UNDERSTANDING
MICHAEL FRAYN

Understanding Contemporary British Literature
Matthew J. Bruccoli, Series Editor

Volumes on

UNDERSTANDING
MICHAEL FRAYN

Merritt Moseley

University of South Carolina Press

© 2006 University of South Carolina

Published by the University of South Carolina Press
Columbia, South Carolina 29208

www.sc.edu/uscpress

Manufactured in the United States of America

15 14 13 12 11 10 09 08 07 06   10 9 8 7 6 5 4 3 2 1

Library of Congress Cataloging-in-Publication Data

Moseley, Merritt, 1949–
   Understanding Michael Frayn / Merritt Moseley.
      p. cm. — (Understanding contemporary British literature)
   Includes bibliographical references (p.   ) and index.
   ISBN-13: 978-1-57003-627-9 (alk. paper)
   ISBN-10: 1-57003-627-6 (alk. paper)
   1. Frayn, Michael—Criticism and interpretation. I. Title. II. Series.
   PR6056.R3Z76 2006
   822'.914—dc22

                                                    2005035451

For my family, with love and appreciation

Contents

Series Editor's Preface

The volumes of *Understanding Contemporary British Literature* have been planned as guides or companions for students as well as good nonacademic readers. The editor and publisher perceive a need for these volumes because much of the influential contemporary literature makes special demands. Uninitiated readers encounter difficulty in approaching works that depart from the traditional forms and techniques of prose and poetry. Literature relies on conventions, but the conventions keep evolving; new writers form their own conventions—which in time may become familiar. Put simply, *UCBL* provides instruction in how to read certain contemporary writers—identifying and explicating their material, themes, use of language, point of view, structures, symbolism, and responses to experience.

The word *understanding* in the titles was deliberately chosen. Many willing readers lack an adequate understanding of how contemporary literature works; that is, what the author is attempting to express and the means by which it is conveyed. Although the criticism and analysis in the series have been aimed at a level of general accessibility, these introductory volumes are meant to be applied in conjunction with the works they cover. They do not provide a substitute for the works and authors they introduce, but rather prepare the reader for more profitable literary experiences.

M. J. B.

Preface

In *The Trick of It,* Michael Frayn's narrator is a literary critic who first specializes in the work of, then marries, a novelist. Doing so proves less satisfactory than he at first expected. It saddens him that he reads all her works and she reads none of his: in other words, that she fails to perceive the equality he would like to claim between the novelist and the critic. And he is finally driven into a competition with her, beginning his own work of fiction. What he cannot seem to find, though, is the trick of it.

There is no discoverable "trick" to writing novels or, for that matter, plays or poems or comic articles. The title *Understanding Michael Frayn,* then, though it announces the purpose of the following book, may be misleading if it suggests either (1) that I have figured out the trick of it or plucked out the mystery of what makes Frayn the writer that he is; or (2) that I believe he is a recondite, nearly inscrutable author whose work will be baffling without my exegesis. His writing is intelligent, witty, philosophical, and learned; but a Michael Frayn novel is not *Finnegans Wake* and does not need a "guide" to bring it within the comprehension of readers. My hope is to contribute some thoughts, drawn from extensive and intensive study of Frayn's writing, that may help increase a reader's insight into, and thus appreciation of, the works.

In writing this book I have benefited, as always, from the supportive environment of my academic home, the University of North Carolina at Asheville, where the librarians are always helpful, teaching loads are sometimes adjusted for writing projects, and the Literature Department comprises a group of good readers and writers, sympathetic and kind, among whom petty academic rivalries (also brilliantly explored in *The Trick of It*) never interfere with productive work. I am thankful for all of these environmental advantages.

The most important environment for me, though, is my family, which sustains me and gives me joy. This book is dedicated to them.

UNDERSTANDING
MICHAEL FRAYN

CHAPTER 1

Introduction
Life and Career

A profile in the *Sunday Times* (London) in 2002 referred to
Michael Frayn as "the giant who bestrides the British arts,"
while hastening to add that he is "a quiet, modest and essentially private man."[1] A survey of his accomplishments since he
began publishing books in 1965 reveals the impressive breadth
of his work. He began his professional writing career in 1957 as
a journalist. His columns in the *Guardian* (Manchester) and
then the *Observer* (London) were primarily comic and satiric,
though founded in serious political and philosophical principles.
In 1965 he wrote his first novel, *The Tin Men;* in 1970 his first
play, *The Two of Us: Four One-Act Plays for Two Players*, was
staged. Alongside thirteen full-length plays and ten novels, he
has written a book of philosophy and has translated many
plays, including all of Chekhov's.

In all of these genres, he has been successful by any standard.
His plays have won the most important prizes available in the
British and American theater, including the Tony Award for Best
Play in the United States (*Copenhagen*) and the Laurence Olivier/
BBC Award for Best New Play in London (*Benefactors*), and
most of them have achieved great popular success as well. *Spies*,
his 2002 novel, was short-listed for the Man Booker Prize for
the best British novel of the year and won the Whitbread Prize
for Best Novel; *Headlong* was also a Booker finalist. Frayn has

won the Heywood Hill Literary Prize, the Somerset Maugham Award, and the Hawthornden Prize. A recent history of the "satire boom" of the 1960s in Britain locates Frayn at the heart of it; and several collections of his early newspaper columns, from as far back as 1959, have been published in paperback and remain in print. Frayn has made documentary films and written screenplays for theatrical movies and television plays.

To call him a "giant bestriding the British arts" may be excessive, yet it is likely that Frayn fails to receive his due in critical judgments of the postwar British literary scene. His own modesty and lack of interest in self-promotion provide one explanation for this state of affairs; his versatility may be another; and the fact that his writing is mostly in the comic vein is undoubtedly a third. For whatever reason, his fiction in particular remains below the horizon of most recent commentators. Jago Morrison's *Contemporary Fiction* (2003) is admittedly a selective study, but while finding room for lengthy treatments of Hanif Kureishi and the hardly contemporary Zora Neale Hurston (who died in 1960), it omits any reference to Frayn; the same is true of Allan Massie's *The Novel Today: A Critical Guide to the British Novel, 1970–1989* and Dominic Head's *The Cambridge Introduction to Modern British Fiction, 1950–2000,* Andrzej Gasiorek's *Post-War British Fiction: Realism and After,* Steven Connor's *The English Novel in History, 1950–1995,* and Patricia Waugh's *The Harvest of the Sixties: English Literature and Its Background, 1960–1990.* Zachary Leader's *On Modern British Fiction* does permit Frayn an appearance in an article on British comic writing, "Between Waugh and Wodehouse," by Christopher Hitchens, who is primarily interested in placing British humorous novelists on a political spectrum. Hitchens characterizes him thus:

Michael Frayn—doggedly and incurably conscience-stricken bleeding-heart liberal; funniest when staying off politics altogether . . . though his masterpiece, *The Tin Men* (1965), flirts with dystopia in satirizing the age of machines and statistics. Frayn is also notable for being the only literary survivor, apart from Alan Bennett, of the 1960s "satire" movement, when the target of ridicule was the stuffy old regime rather than the canons of levelling and self-pitying political correctness.[2]

Malcolm Bradbury includes Michael Frayn in a list of authors who "practiced the art of skeptical and critical comedy," and acknowledges them, perhaps faintly, as providing a relief to "the end-of-the-world news, the catastrophic gloom, the disaster vision."[3]

Frayn's work in the theater has attracted considerably more critical attention than have his novels. Insofar as academic critics have written about his work (which is not to suggest that academic criticism is the measure of success that Frayn would pine for), it has been his plays they consider; and among the plays, very much the majority of the criticism is devoted to two: *Noises Off* (1982) and *Copenhagen* (1998). Christopher Innes treats Frayn's stage work alongside that of Alan Ayckbourn, calling them the two playwrights "who set the tone for popular comedy during the eighties."[4] He further suggests that their "emphasis on entertainment also leads to their work being generally undervalued, in removing it from the sphere of academic criticism, which tends to measure the significance of drama by intellectual content or political commitment" (313). Undoubtedly Innes is right in his diagnosis, though the unreflective implication that entertainment is in some way inconsistent with intellectual content or political commitment is problematic.

Perhaps it would be more accurate to say that many critics cannot imagine that a work can be intellectually or politically serious without foregoing laughter. Michael Billington, theater critic for the *Guardian,* takes a more independent view of Frayn: "He smuggles ideas into commercially popular forms. His plays are serious comedies about people's attempts to interpret the world, about the constant battle between the forces of order and disorder, about the search for happiness."[5]

Somewhere between "the giant who bestrides the British arts" and "a perfectly agreeable boulevarde writer, but not as serious as people claim," in Giles Gordon's words[6]—and closer to the first judgment—is probably the right placement of Michael Frayn in the world of contemporary British writing. Frank Rich ably sums up his claims to the attention of readers and theatergoers:

> He seems to me a contemporary Renaissance man. He brings the same meticulousness to a great variety of theatrical forms, from "Noises Off" to a philosophical play like "Clouds," to the knotty puzzle of reconstructing a play like [Chekhov's] "Platonov." He's serious in the best sense, both in perfecting the mechanics that go into making a farce and in facing the big issues, like the decline of liberalism. And he's interested in other forms, too—journalism, the novel, metaphysical discussion, everything.[7]

Similarly, Blake Morrison points to Frayn's distinctiveness:

> With nearly everybody you can think that they're primarily a novelist or primarily a playwright, but Michael's genuinely, equally both. And there are two sides to him, in both the theater and fiction. On the one hand he has a real taste for farce, but he's also a very serious-minded man, with an almost

dry academic temperament and a slightly professorial look about him.[8]

And Philip Hensher, an intelligent observer of the British literary scene, believes that Frayn is

> so remarkable because, underneath the supremely accomplished, almost boulevard technique and inventiveness, he always gently and respectfully invites his audience to contemplate some extremely knotty concepts. He knows, in short, what he is doing; and he trusts you to listen.[9]

The Michael Frayn described by these commentators has grown out of an ordinary life history that gives, at first glance, no promise of his later accomplishments.

Life

Michael Frayn is a Londoner. He was born September 8, 1933, above a wine shop in Mill Hill, a northern suburb. His father, Thomas Allen Frayn, was an asbestos salesman, his mother, Violet Alice Lawson Frayn, a shop assistant and sometime model (Frayn retains in his office a picture of her modeling for Harrod's). He places his social status, somewhat uncertainly, on the borders of lower-middle and middle-middle class.[10] When Michael was eighteen months old, his family moved to Ewell, another London suburb, this one south of the center. He attended a fee-paying private school, the Sutton High School for Boys, until, when he was thirteen, his mother died. The death of his mother was emotionally difficult for him; further, it strained his family's financial circumstances, and he was placed in Kingston Grammar School—selective and academic, but state-supported. He has spoken of how awful his private school was—claiming that its headmaster, a clergyman, began each day by beating twenty boys. Awful it may have been, but it was a private school, and about moving to the state sector, he has said, "Although I was suspicious at first that something terrible was going on somewhere, in fact it saved me."[11] At Kingston Grammar he wrote poetry, edited a magazine, and formed a Communist cell with a classmate. A good student, he earned a place at Emmanuel College, Cambridge, and a state scholarship.

But before his matriculation, he chose to complete the national (military) service then required of all young men. He was named to a place on Dame Elizabeth Hill's Joint Services course for military interpreters at Cambridge, where he studied Russian. Another member of the unit was Alan Bennett, who would become famous first as a member of the *Beyond the Fringe* troupe and then as a successful playwright; the two became good friends and wrote sketches together. Frayn loved his time at Cambridge, and his Russian studies were obviously to prove useful in his translations of Chekhov's plays.

In 1954 he entered Cambridge University. Initially he read French and Russian, but after a year he changed his focus to moral sciences, a course now known as philosophy. He could not help being affected by the famous Cambridge philosopher of the time, Ludwig Wittgenstein, who died three years before Frayn came up to Cambridge but still exercised an enormous influence on the philosophy faculty. Frayn says that he was "one of the world's greatest philosophers, but he was also a terrible human being, an appalling bully, who terrified everyone on the faculty" except for Frayn's own supervisor, who helped him escape the Wittgenstein influence.[12] There are, as observant readers have pointed out, significant philosophical concerns in many of Frayn's novels and plays, and he wrote a book of philosophical speculation, or aperçus, called *Constructions* in 1974. As a Cambridge undergraduate he wrote for *Granta*, the university's literary magazine, and for Footlights, the annual Cambridge student revue. Traditionally, a Footlights show is transferred to a West End production in London; Frayn's *Zounds!* was not, and this disappointment may have delayed the beginning of his career as a playwright: his first play was produced in 1970. His Communist sympathies had not lasted and, he says, "vanished in 1956," when he and four Cambridge friends visited the Soviet Union on an unofficial exchange.[13]

Upon graduation in 1957, Frayn took a job with the *Guardian*, one of the nation's major daily newspapers, then still called the *Manchester Guardian*. It was a good first job for him, though he was unhappy about having to live in Manchester. He reported news from the north of England and the metropolis and did some reviewing. Because he knew Russian, he was assigned to cover Harold Macmillan's trip to Moscow. (Though his belief in Communism was behind him by this time, he remained interested in Russian, and Soviet, affairs.)

His career took its most significant step forward when, in 1959, he was put in charge of a humorous column, "Miscellany." Frayn recalls the column's beginnings: "in those far-off days there were very few of us doing it, and the appearance of a column in the papers occasioned almost as much curiosity and mirth as the sight of a horseless carriage in the streets."[14] His column at first appeared three times a week; after three years he transferred it to the *Observer*, a Sunday newspaper, where naturally it appeared only once a week, for another six years.

> Governments came and fell. Sex was invented. Novel intoxicants were tried. Things were protested against. Two hundred and thirty five of these columns were reprinted in four

> books that appeared at the time (*The Day of the Dog, The Book of Fub, On the Outskirts* and *At Bay in Gear Street*). The rest were put to good use lighting fires or wrapping fish-heads for the cat, and have not been heard of since.[15]

Frayn's self-deprecating account understates both the influence of these columns and their staying power.

Though there is considerable debate about the so-called satire boom of the 1960s, the term does refer to a real collection of phenomena, undoubtedly including the production of *Beyond the Fringe*—a long-running stage play, in London and New York, starring Alan Bennett, Peter Cook, Dudley Moore, and Jonathan Miller—as well as the launching of *Private Eye,* a satirical fortnightly, and possibly the television show *That Was the Week That Was.* Humphrey Carpenter's history of the movement quotes the *Observer*'s account of the new *Private Eye:* "It is run by a disorganized staff just down from Oxbridge, helped by eight pretty girls. . . . Their hero is Michael Frayn. . . . Their main job, they feel, is to attack hypocrisy and ineffi-ciency."[16] There was an unsuccessful attempt to dramatize Frayn's *Guardian* columns for *That Was the Week That Was.* Frayn has never seemed wholly happy to be considered a satirist or credited with the satire boom. Carpenter quotes him as say-ing, about his newspaper columns, "I suppose there were satiri-cal elements in my column. . . . Maybe there were the beginnings of that slightly disrespectful tone" (118). Uneasily, he admits that "we who were involved with 'satire' in the 1960s may all have been partially responsible for the fact that there is now [1999] a tone in a lot of the press of a permanent sneer at almost everything, which is very depressing" (329).

The columns have not dated badly, despite the changing times and the loss of many period references. James Fenton insists that Frayn's "virtues as a comic writer were always based on an ability to evoke the instantly recognizable—the awful predicament, the common foible, the typical character. He is the funniest journalist of our time, and he is also the master of comic form. These are not merely sustained jokes. They are model essays."[17] Fenton's comments come in his introduction to a collection of pieces chosen from Frayn's *Guardian* and *Observer* columns, collected from the four book-length collections and *Observer* columns not previously published in book form. *The Original Michael Frayn* appeared in 1983. In 1986 *Jarvis's Frayn,* a selection of thirty-one columns, was recorded by Martin Jarvis and went out over BBC Radio 4.

In 1994 Frayn went back to writing a column in the *Guardian,* and the resulting thirty-two columns, along with a few others published elsewhere, or nowhere, appeared in *Speak after the Beep* (1997); then a further collection, including all the *Speak after the Beep* columns and some others, was published as *The Additional Michael Frayn* in 2000. Clearly readers' appetite for his journalistic pieces, some of them written almost forty years earlier, had not disappeared.

But this was a reversion—as Frayn says, "I slipped into my old ways"[18]—rather than a continuation. Indeed, he had abandoned the regular column in 1968. James Fenton suggests that the form had "lost its attraction."[19] One account Frayn has provided is simply, "I wanted to write novels but couldn't do it while writing three columns a week. So when the *Observer* offered one column a week I took it. But although I knew I wanted to write books, I was very cautious in the way I did it. I went on writing the column for five years." He even calls his first novel, *The Tin Men,* "something of an interim work between a column and a novel."[20] He did tell Benedict Nightingale that he was growing uneasy with the malice of the satire boom: "I very much dislike the side of myself I discovered when I first began to be a humorist."[21]

He began as a columnist and novelist; after five years of writing and publishing novels, and with the momentum provided by writing scripts for television, he switched to plays. Though it would be overly schematic to insist that he has been only novelist or playwright in strict and exclusive alternation, his career has gone through phases when he was only writing fiction, others when he wrote only plays. He maintains that ideas for books come to him with their genre decided rather than fitting into a plan of his own for what he will do next.

The Tin Men appeared in 1965. Having begun writing novels, he wrote them quickly and successfully: *The Russian Interpreter* followed in 1966, *Towards the End of the Morning* in 1967, and *A Very Private Life* in 1968; then, after a longer hiatus during which he began a successful career as a playwright, *Sweet Dreams* was published in 1973. That was his last novel for sixteen years. His abandonment of prose fiction seems related to problems of voice. He told Benedict Nightingale, "I found it more and more difficult to know what my own voice was, and was more and more tempted by the opportunity of just hearing the voices of the characters" (128). Having given voice to many different characters in his dramatic works, when he wrote another novel, *The Trick of It,* in 1989, he found using a first-person narrator a sufficiently dramatic device to solve the problem of authorial voice.

In 1968 Michael Frayn, by then a highly successful columnist, was asked to contribute to "an evening of short plays about marriage" (128). The impresario who had commissioned the play rejected it as "filthy." Frayn explains, "I was so incensed that I wrote three more two-character plays of my own, and they came into the West End under the title, 'The Two of Us.' It was a critical catastrophe, but it managed to run nine months" (128). *The Two of Us: Four One-Act Plays*, his first West End play, was produced in 1970 (he had written television scripts that had been televised in 1968 and 1969). In his introduction to *Plays: 2*, he states flatly:

> You can classify plays in any number of ways—as comedies or tragedies; as verse or prose, as high comedies, low comedies, black comedies, tragic-comedies; as art or entertainment. But however you do it they all fall into two even more fundamental categories—they are all hits or flops.[22]

Most of Michael Frayn's plays have been hits, to some degree. Between *The Two of Us* (1970) and *Look Look* (1990), he had eight of his own original plays and nine translations staged. One particularly fruitful year, 1975, saw the premieres of *Alphabetical Order, Donkeys' Years,* and *Clouds*. His biggest hit of these years was *Noises Off,* which made its appearance in 1982.

Things changed rather abruptly with *Look Look* in 1990. Nicholas Wroe refers to *Look Look* as a "catastrophic flop."[23] It ran for twenty-seven performances, and Frayn recounts, "until we played our first preview everyone thought we had a hit. That day it became quite clear that we in fact had a corpse."[24] In an interview with Marcy Kahan, he said, "My career went into a considerable decline, particularly in the theater, after the failure of *Look Look*. And the next two plays I did didn't do as badly as *Look Look* but they didn't arouse much interest. And I was certainly expecting to face downwards into oblivion and was very surprised when things turned around a bit with *Copenhagen* [produced in 1998] and *Headlong* [published in 1999]."[25]

During a period of relative obscurity in his theatrical career, however, Frayn had returned to fiction. *The Trick of It* (1989) actually preceded *Look Look*. It was followed by *A Landing on the Sun* (1991), *Now You Know* (1992), *Headlong* (1999), and *Spies* (2002). Observers often noticed the triumphant conjunction of *Copenhagen,* a great hit in London and New York, and *Headlong,* which was a major critical success, short-listed for both the Booker and Whitbread prizes in Britain. Admiring profiles recognize his impressive work rate. He told the *Sunday Times* in 2002, "Each year I say I'll work less hard, and each year I seem to work harder. . . . And if you haven't got a job, which I haven't, it's very difficult to retire, isn't it?"[26]

Michael Frayn was married in 1960 to Gillian Palmer. They lived in southeast London and for a time were involved in a cooperative housing scheme that provided some of the material inspiration for his play *Benefactors*. They had three daughters, Jenny, Susanna, and Rebecca. In the early 1980s Michael met writer and biographer Claire Tomalin at a meeting of a satirical lunch club, called the Society for the Discouragement of Public Relations, and left his wife for her. In 1989 Frayn and Palmer divorced, and in 1993 he and Claire Tomalin were married. Their marriage has attracted considerable press commentary—for instance, the suggestion that they are "Britain's premiere literary couple"[27]—particularly after the announcement, in 2002, that Frayn's *Spies* and Tomalin's *Samuel Pepys* had both been nominated for Whitbread Book Awards; he won the best novel award and she the best biography, thus pitting them against each other for the Whitbread Book of the Year Award. Claire Tomalin won.

In 2003 the *Sunday Times* discovered and published a list of distinguished people who had been offered honors by Tony Blair's Labour government but had rejected them, and it included both Michael Frayn and Claire Tomalin. As in the 2002 Whitbread judging, Claire Tomalin came out slightly on top, having refused a CBE (Companion of the British Empire), while Frayn's rejected honor was a knighthood.[28]

Overview

In interviews Michael Frayn often deplores the diversity of his output. To the interviewer from the *Paris Review,* for instance, he insisted in 2003:

> Let me say for a start that I don't think it is a very good idea to write different sorts of things. If I were to give serious practical advice to a young writer about how to succeed I would say: "Write the same book, or the same play, over and over again, just very slightly different, so that people get used to it. It takes some time, but if you do it often enough, finally people will get the hang of it, and get familiar with it, and they'll like it. Then you go on producing a consistent product and you'll have a market for it." . . . If I could have done this, I would have.[29]

Considering the length, versatility, complexity, and multifarious successfulness of Frayn's career, a career that flouts the canny advice he offers to other writers, efforts to sum him up are probably doomed to failure. This has not prevented people from making such efforts.

Frayn, though he submits to interviews frequently, especially (of course) when he has a new book or play out or is nominated for an award, is a reserved man, sparing of grand self-analyses. Nevertheless, he has told Benedict Nightingale that the subject of his dramatic work—at least up to *Benefactors*—is "the way we impose our own ideas on the world around us"; and he has commented to Robert McCrum that "the truth about life is that people often don't behave with dignity. They do get confused. Events turn out to be confusing. People don't always behave with the gravitas one might like them to behave with. I think my characters tend to go that way."[30] A disposition to write about people doing real jobs and a conviction that "the great world of work in which we all live could be represented on the stage"— which includes activities ranging from managing the database at a newspaper to running an open-access lobby, working at a trade show selling room dividers to conducting an espionage campaign against West Germany—is a testament to the side of Michael Frayn that values common sense and common values.[31] It is important to register how seldom, in his long and fertile career, he has written about characters who, like him, are writers or intellectuals. Frayn's two self-observations above are more "philosophical": the summary provided to Nightingale, epistemological, and the one to McCrum, ethical; and they remind the reader of the continuing philosophical concerns that may be glimpsed in nearly everything he writes.

Julia Llewellyn Smith diagnoses:

> In all Frayn's work, from *Clockwise,* his film starring John Cleese, to *Spies,* the recurring theme is chaos. The most logical plans are upstaged by events. Intellect offers no protection against late-running trains or lost contact lenses.

"I'm trying to make sense of the world around me," he protests. "There's no other way of doing it. I wouldn't make any claim for understanding the world better than people who don't write, but you do have to think why things happen, and it does bring you up against very big questions and you have to think very hard."[32]

Philip Hensher argues with equal power the contrasting view that

Frayn's principal subject from the start, I think, has been the more or less anguished relations people have with language. Put like that, it sounds like an austere sort of interest, but Frayn has perceived that here lies not just a rich seam of philosophical inquiry, but an inexhaustible source of preposterous comic invention. Conventionally, one says that he is interested in the ways people use language, but it would be more accurate to say that his subject in the way language uses people.[33]

There is evidence of this concern from the early columns, in which he skillfully parodies the Bible and Shakespeare, or the language of the professional interview, or the strained journalese of American publications reporting on "Swinging London," as well as in his 2002 novel, *Spies,* where the protagonist's failure to understand the dark suggestion that "the Juice" is living in his neighborhood is both comic and tragic.

Christopher Hitchens approaches Frayn's work more through class. He writes that his "preferred raw material is the status anxiety, and vulnerability to embarrassment, of the *bien-pensant* middle class. (Together with the late cartoonist Marc Boxer, he has in effect been the chronicler of this anxious and energetic stratum, with its gnawing guilts and worries about private schooling, the environment, and multiculturalism.)"[34] Like any such totalizing statement, Hitchens's is partly wrong, as a consideration of *Copenhagen* (about atomic physicists in Denmark during World War II) or *Sweet Dreams* (a vision of the hereafter) will attest. He continues, though, to identify Frayn's chief theme as "authenticity and the difficulty of deciding it," which goes beyond class anxiety to the mysteries of identity (and language, for that matter).

Claire Armitstead points to Frayn's sympathies with Chekhov —he is the foremost English translator of the Russian playwright—and points out that each of them is "a polymath who did his time as a professional humorist. But," she cautions, "to describe him as Chekhovian is to ignore the feature that unites his oeuvre, and sets it apart from anyone else's: he is first and foremost a journalist, with a reporter's ability to smell a story and then research it and find the right form for it."[35] This neat formulation must be qualified, both by Frayn's own frequent protestations that he dislikes doing the research that underlies his plays and, more crucially, by the fact that he was a journalist in Armitstead's sense for no more than three years; it was his disinclination to pursue stories and dig out the research that led to his more fanciful creations.

Like any good writer, Michael Frayn resists pigeonholing. The closest summary of his work to completeness may be the statement that he is a comic writer; but, having said this, one immediately thinks of contradictory examples. Though he told one interviewer that the secret of success is to do the same thing again and again, he has followed a very different career path, one marked by originality and willingness to change, as well as generic and thematic versatility. Ian McEwan declares, "I still don't think Frayn's full measure has been properly taken by the wider reading public. In some ways he reminds me of [Jorge Luis] Borges because of the intellectual playfulness, but he is far less dry than Borges and much more caught up in the everyday. Like all good writers, in the end he's on his own."[36]

CHAPTER 2

Journalism, Translations, and Miscellaneous Nonfiction

Michael Frayn's early work for the *Manchester Guardian*, consisting of no-longer-timely reporting, no longer survives outside of old files. He worked on "'color pieces'—usually a personal essay about some Northern folkway, the last handloom weaver in Bolton, or the last lock maker in Westhoughton."[1] When he began writing the Miscellany column in 1959 he began to produce literature that lasts.

The book publication of these columns was chronological; as he accumulated enough columns, a selection from them would appear as a book. *The Day of the Dog* (1962) was a collection of columns that had appeared in the *Guardian* before that point; *The Book of Fub* (1963, published in the United States under the title *Never Put Off to Gomorrah . . .*) reprinted more periodical pieces from the same paper; *On the Outskirts* (1964) and *At Bay in Gear Street* (1967) followed, printing selections from the *Observer* column. When *The Original Michael Frayn* appeared in 1983, it collected a narrowed selection from these first four books and added nineteen further *Observer* columns that had appeared after *At Bay in Gear Street* and had not previously been published in a book. Some of these early columns were also collected in *Listen to This: Sketches and Monologues* (1990).[2] An omnibus volume, this book included some sketches written for a television series starring Eleanor Bron ("Beyond a Joke," BBC2, 1972) as well as some content from *On the*

Outskirts and *The Book of Fub*. Notable in this collection are a set of skits with recurring characters, three sons who while visiting their mother pay no attention to each other and compete in windy and pompous pronouncements about such matters as house prices and driving itineraries. These were originally newspaper sketches written in play form, and they easily adapt for staging.

After a long pause, Frayn went back to a weekly column in 1994. As he explained it, "I wrote a regular column when I was a young man for a number of years. Then I stopped. I stopped because I didn't want to grow old and find I was still at the start of another piece."[3] He likened his return to a weekly column to an alcoholic's backsliding, and stopped again after thirty-three columns. Almost all of these were published in 1995 as *Speak after the Beep: Studies in the Art of Communicating with Inanimate and Semi-Animate Objects,* and in 1996 they were broadcast on BBC Radio 4. In 2000, obviously responding to an unsatisfied demand, Frayn brought out *The Additional Michael Frayn,* which reprinted the pieces from *Speak after the Beep,* one new (1999) column from the *Guardian,* and nineteen previously uncollected *Guardian* and *Observer* pieces.

Given this history, it seems simplest to discuss the comic journalism thematically rather than chronologically. Frayn's columns are often personal, though they reveal more about a dramatized persona than about the author's true biography. They also reveal a sort of parallel world occupied by a recurring cast of fictional characters; there is much in the way of parody; there is considerable literary commentary, as one would expect from Michael Frayn; and there are political columns, though these are not as frequent as one might expect in the *Guardian,* a newspaper then strongly associated with the Labour party.

Frayn's presentation of himself in his columns as an average man, coping with the ordinary challenges of modern life with difficulty, helps to explain why several observers have called his column Thurberesque. In the column "Fun with Numbers," for instance, the subject is the difficulty of memorizing one's four-digit code for the ATM machine. "Wine Is a Mocker" begins with this declaration: "A man who has suffered more anxiety and embarrassment with supercilious waiters in expensive restaurants than I have would be difficult to find."[4] Introducing a column on the anxiety that arises from suspecting that other people know sophisticated things that one has missed, he writes:

> I think I can take it as generally agreed that every human being has an inalienable right to enjoy a decent inferiority complex, and that, if we are going to have a healthy nation, society must be so arranged that everyone is just behind someone else in the race, to enable us to keep our weight down and maintain our nervous system in high tone.[5]

Elsewhere Frayn frets about the realization (delivered by his first wife, then a sociology student) that journalists are lower-middle class; he will accept being designated middle class, or working class, or upper-lower-middle, but not the one that, according to some faceless government taxonomist, he inhabits. In a column that eventually turns to calling for an end to agreeing with fashionable moral judgments because fashions change, he gives as an example the fashion of laughing at the suburbs—such as those in which he grew up—"The idea of actually *describing* the suburbs, without either laughing at them or moralizing about them, evidently seems to most people about as far-fetched as mapping a plate of mashed potato."[6]

The predominant note of the personal essays is worry—in the early essays, from the 1960s, worry about choosing the right title, knowing the right things, belonging to the right class stratum, living in the right place. Later essays often involve worry about technology (particularly those collected as *Speak after the Beep*); for instance, one of them complains about the simultaneous failure of the fax machine, telephone, and television, and provides rueful suggestions for how the author could have prevented it—"I shouldn't have kept making the fax and the copier read things I'd written."[7]

Related to the personal, quasi-autobiographical columns are the sizable number populated by fictional characters. Some of them figure as Frayn intimates, like the Crumbles and the Morrises. They represent niches slightly above and slightly below the Frayns, and play their parts in a continuing mockery of intellectual and social fashion seeking. As Frayn explained it in 2000:

> I had two couples in the column, Christopher and Lavinia Crumble, and Horace and Doris Morris. Christopher and Lavinia Crumble knew more than I did, and were much cleverer than me, and used to patronize me. And Horace and Doris Morris were stupider than me and I patronized them. So I would find out from Christopher and Lavinia Crumble what the smart ideas of the day were, and I then would go and be astonished that Horace and Doris Morris didn't know about them.[8]

Beyond these are what Nicholas Wroe calls "a beguiling cast of 60's archetypes":[9] fictional people like Christopher Smoothe, a Conservative backbencher, later Minister of Chance and Spec; Nigel Sharpe-Groomsman, a Tory Member of Parliament; Rollo Swavely, a public relations consultant; Sir Harold Sidewinder, the well-known chairman and man of opinion; T. Spencer Up-creep and his wife Mary; the Bishop of Twicester (pronounced "twister"); Rock Richmond, a popular rock-and-roll singer; and George Snugg, Member of Parliament for the Isle of Dogs. Snugg is a Labour politician, but Labour is satirized consider-ably less than the Conservative party, the explanation for which probably combines Frayn's own political beliefs with the fact that the Conservatives were in power through most of the 1960s. Special targets are public relations, greedy speculators, heartless politicians, and all varieties of cant. In one essay he responds to the Bishop of Woolwich, a controversial clergyman of the times, whose book *Honest to God* (1963) deplored super-naturalism, called belief in heaven an obstacle to faith, and was perceived as part of the "Death of God" movement. Frayn invents a mass rally of OIGMGO—the "Our Image of God Must Go Movement"—convened by the progressive divine, the Bishop of Twicester, and attended by "Rollo Swavely (the well-known public relations consultant) and Rock Richmond (the eminent teenager)."[10]

Frayn was in good company with these fanciful creations. Perhaps the best-known (and probably longest-running) humor-ous newspaper column in Britain was the Beachcomber column in the *Daily Express* (London), written by J. B. Morton for over fifty years; for forty-one years it appeared six times a week. Morton's regular characters included Dr. Strabismus, Dr. Smart-Allick of Narkover School, Captain Foulenough, Prodnose, and a judge called Mr. Justice Cocklecarrot. This name is still in use in *Private Eye* (a publication associated, like Frayn, with the satire boom), the founders of which were very much influenced by Beachcomber (the *Private Eye* logo parodies that of the *Daily Express*). The Peter Simple column in the London *Daily*

Telegraph (like the *Express,* a conservative newspaper) uses the same devices, including such characters as Julian Birdbath (a literary scholar), Dr. Spacely-Trellis, the Bishop of Sketchford, and so on. *Private Eye* itself has long featured such recurrent characters, including journalist Lunchtime O'Booze and football manager Ron Knee, of Neasden Football Club, with its two supporters, Sid and Doris Bonkers, and its one-legged star striker, Baldy Pevsner.

Among the features of modern life Frayn parodies are some very deserving ones like party political broadcasts, instruction manuals, and travel books. He sometimes writes in a Biblical style, as, for example, when targeting Kwame Nkrumah's Nigeria or the use of "get with it" in publicity campaigns. He has a brilliant spoof of flippant television listings, in the form of a history of the world with thumbnail blurbs like "The Council of Trent. Predictable ecclesiastical romp."[11] In "The Mails Must Go Through," he satirizes familiar letter writing: two sisters-in-law exchange a correspondence empty of almost all content except for excuses for not writing earlier, excuses for not writing longer letters, and vague and meaningless assurances of good health. In "At Bay in Gear Street," he makes fun of American journalists' frenzy over "Swinging London"; Frayn represents himself as having been assaulted by a pack of correspondents in Carnaby Street who identify him as "actor Terry Stamp, 26, in mini-wig and P.V.C. spectacles!" and his wife as "diminutive dolly Cathy McGowan, 22, in an eight-inches-above-the-knee, Campari-red skirtlet, spectre-pale make-up, and kinky wobble-as-you-walk celluloid eyelids!"[12] When asked about supposed members of his circle—Leslie Caron, photographer David Bailey, and Lady Jane Ormsby-Gore—he replies that "the circle I moved in . . . consisted of Christopher and Lavinia

Crumble, Horace and Doris Morris, and people like that," setting the life-style journalists off on a mad quest for that new
scene, which promises "entirely fresh dimensions of fabness"
and "the hope of a whole gear universe of prime-quality groovi-
ness!"[13]

Frayn's most interesting parodies are of the forms he was, or
would become, most familiar with. Frayn had done some inter-
viewing as a journalist, as well as giving many celebrity interviews since achieving success as a playwright. In "'I Do Have
One Pet Hate,' He Laughed," he claims that "the interview is
the major art form of the era";[14] in "I Think I'm Right in Saying," he proposes that the interview has replaced both writing
and oratory. Some recent interviewers of Frayn still acknowledge his early satire of the form, "Behind the Myth—Mythtier
Still," a celebrity interview of a man famous for playing the
front legs of film monsters. The tone is perfectly captured:

> You ring the bell, and when the door opens you walk inside.
> "I'm afraid Mr. Tramplin's still in the bath," says someone.
> You note the remark down. You've come to do a cultural
> interview for a highbrow publication, and you have a lot of
> space to fill. You sit down to wait in a respectful attitude. You
> assume your readers will guess that when you say you you
> mean not they but I.[15]

Frayn also satirizes novels, including the novels of the "Mete-
orological School"—novels that begin with the weather—but
his most interesting literary satire is of the theater. In one column about television, he identifies it as ranking "somewhere
above the theatre but below the yo-yo";[16] in another, "Black
Whimsy," he announces a mail-order course in writing black
comedy, in which his primary target seems to be the early plays

of Harold Pinter. It contains such advice as this: "The trick is to think of the stereotype—to think of the cliché character, the cliché reaction—and then WRITE EXACTLY THE OPPOSITE!"[17] His most scathing comment on theater, "Please Keep All Exits Clear," begins by declaring that "just about the least pleasant way of spending an evening there is, short of standing in the rain without a coat on, is to go to the theatre."[18] This is in part because of the stupid behavior of fellow theater-goers, but then there is the deadly predictability of the play itself:

> I think it's the set, with the warm afternoon floodlight falling on the lace curtains at the french windows, and the three steps up to a landing along which some well-known middle-aged actress is going to make an applauded entrance in about fifteen minutes' time. Unless it's the knowledge that very soon a door is going to open and shut, with the specially thin noise a stage door makes when it opens and shuts, disgorging one of the more junior members off the cast, who will rearrange the cushions, pour a drink, pick up a newspaper, or labour some other wordless byplay until another character arrives to start the dialogue which dexterously establishes that the heroine, who has two precocious children, is about to give a dinner party for her first husband and her second husband's mistress.[19]

Frayn generously goes on to acknowledge that "only about thirty-eight of the forty-one theatres in London are still staging plays like this" and then provides pastiches of two other types: the gloomy kitchen-sink drama about "a self-confessed whore at seventeen . . . still carrying on her activities though in failing health and mentality" and an alteration of that depressing scenario into an Irish play, set in "Oirland during the

Thrubbles" and full of bagpipe music and a chorus of IRA men.[20] This may be an example of what the author meant when he said that after his Cambridge Footlights revue failed, "I reacted in a sour-grapes way against the theater. . . . I hated the theater. Then very slowly I went back to it."[21]

But Frayn's satire, despite its inventiveness, frequent brilliance, and undoubted comedy, is a humane variety, and he deplores his more savage counterparts. In "Strength through Joy" he powerfully satirizes the satire boom itself, or its pretensions, in an account of a rally of the "National Satirical Movement." His point is to critique the jeering, cruel tone of much satire, as one speaker exults:

> "A year or two ago, if we had ridiculed a man for being a drunk, or writing a flop, or having a detached retina, all the namby-pamby do-gooders would have whined. But nowadays everybody joins in the fun. Or at least looks the other way. Perhaps they are afraid of being hauled off and satirized themselves as the namby-pamby do-gooders that they are.
>
> "It is strange now to think that our movement started by appealing to men's intelligence and sense of justice to laugh at injustice and stupidity. How limited that appeal was! How much more universal and powerful is our appeal to men's malice, resentment, destructiveness, and envy!"[22]

Add suffering and inequality to injustice and stupidity as proper objects of satire and one gets an idea of the political values Frayn's satirical columns demonstrate. This humaneness and distaste for cruelty are marks of his entire career. Larissa MacFarquhar points out the "absence of bile" in his work. "Nowhere is there the contempt for small vanities, the scorn for failure, the sour relishing of pride brought low, the bitter spitting at the greed and selfishness and viciousness of the world that are inescapable in most serious fiction of the past two hundred years."[23] Obviously some of the Christopher Smoothe and Nigel Sharpe-Groomsman MP material is anti-Tory satire, focusing on ethical blindness and materialism. In other essays, he writes in a more overtly heartfelt (though still indirect) way about those values that really matter. In one early column, "The Companions of the Right Hand," the premise is that right-wing columnists always know what "so-called progressives" are going to think. For instance, "'Foreseeably,' they yawn, 'self-styled liberal intellectuals are in a high state of self-righteous indignation about the two West Indians who were thrown out of an all-white plane over the Atlantic yesterday. . . . The employment of children in mines, on which this country's economic survival depends, will no doubt elicit a typically stereotyped response from "enlightened" opinion. . . . The usual progressive parrot cries will now of course be heard calling for a ban on advertising thumb-screws and mantraps.'"[24]

Some thirty years later he reacted to the new terms "luvvie" and "chattering classes," commonly used in the media for actors and intellectuals of progressive views, by affecting to worry about becoming a luvvie and canvassing the symptoms of that disorder.

> The first symptom is that you're sitting there in a reasonably warm room, with food on the table in front of you, and a glass of wine, and you feel some faint spasm of sympathy passing through you for some other group of human beings, who as a result of their own fecklessness, or through the operation of natural laws beyond your control, are not sitting in a reasonably warm room, with food and a glass of wine in front of them . . . when suddenly, out of nowhere, you hear

this terrible . . . thing coming out of your mouth. This pious, sententious, canting, do-gooding, expression of hypocritical concern for someone not yourself.[25]

The rest of the column provides remedies for those who may detect symptoms in themselves of being luvvies.

If it is possible to sum up the Michael Frayn who appears in these essays, besides saying that he is funny and clever and inventive and erudite, the keys are in the values implied above—a humane appreciation of other people's claims to attention, an antipathy to cruelty, and a genuine modesty.

Translations

Beginning in the late 1970s with an invitation from the National Theatre to translate Tolstoy's *The Fruits of Enlightenment* and Chekhov's *The Cherry Orchard,* Michael Frayn has constructed an impressive record as a translator, mostly from the Russian. Characteristically, he has explained this in a self-deprecating way, claiming that those other writers who knew Russian could not write plays and those who could write plays did not know Russian. These are his translated plays with the dates of their English premieres: *The Cherry Orchard* (1978); *The Fruits of Enlightenment* (1979); *Number One* (a translation from the French of Anouilh, 1978); Chekhov's *Wild Honey* (a translation of an untitled play usually called "Platonov," 1984), *Three Sisters* (1985), *The Seagull* (1986), *The Sneeze* (a compilation of sketches and short fictions, 1988), *Uncle Vanya* (1988); and *The Exchange* (translated and adapted from Yuri Trifonov, 1989). During much of this period he had two of his translated plays running at the same time. Several of these opened at the National Theatre; others at less imposing venues like the

Nuffield Theatre, Southampton, or the Palace Theatre, Watford, though they might later transfer to the West End. His Chekhov translations were well received in New York as well as London, and they have become recognized as the standard translations for most productions. A fellow translator, Jack Laskowski, calls his work on Chekhov "as close to perfection in the translator's art as it is possible to get."[26]

Despite his work on Anouilh, Tolstoy, or Trifonov, Frayn clearly has an affinity for Chekhov, so much so that commentators have regularly called him Chekhovian. His own long and thoughtful introduction to the Methuen anthology of his translations suggests three similarities between the two writers. Chekhov was not a natural dramatist and started out "as a humorist in the comic journals";[27] moreover, according to Frayn, Chekhov is interested, in an unprecedented way, in showing people working on stage: *The Seagull* "is surely the first great theatrical classic where we see the principals set about the ordinary, humdrum business of their lives" (xv). Work is one of Frayn's particular interests in his writing, too. Finally, there is the question of how Chekhov's plays are to be read—are they comedies or even "vaudevilles" (Frayn's description), or are they melodramas or even tragedies? Frayn's work has not produced the same confusions as Chekhov's, but reception of his work has sometimes calcified into a conviction that a play is funny, or it is serious—in which case it shouldn't be funny.

There is a difference between translating a play and adapting it, or producing a "version" of it. In recent years, probably because so few playwrights are fluent in another language, the theater has accommodated many plays somehow rendered into English by playwrights who do not know the language the plays were composed in. Tom Stoppard's "version" of Ferenc Molnar's *Rough Crossing,* Pam Gems's, David Hare's, and David Lan's versions of Chekhov, and many others are by English writers who cannot adequately read the language of the original. Frayn, who is fluent in Russian, has admitted to finding this practice "very irritating" and says he wouldn't dream of writing a version of a play from a language he couldn't read.[28] Ironically, his reservations were not shared by his original producers; the National Theatre invited him to translate Tolstoy's *Fruits of Enlightenment* without realizing that he knew Russian.[29]

In at least two cases, his work on a play has gone beyond faithful translation. Frayn's *Wild Honey* is his adaptation and translation of a mysterious play by Chekhov, never performed in his lifetime and left untitled by the loss of its first page. Called "Platonov" after its main character, it is an undisciplined work —scholars appear to agree that it is Chekhov's earliest full-length play—that would run for six hours if uncut. Frayn cut and rearranged it, discarding some elements while leaving the plot and the relationships—particularly those between the romantic Platonov and the four women who are his lovers— intact. He explained:

> I tried to write Chekhov's play for him. . . . I didn't try to make it my own play. Nor did I try to make it like any of Chekhov's later plays, because he was a young, very different playwright when he wrote it. I tried to make that play work as a play. And I decided that the only way to do this was to assume that the original text was a rough draft and could be treated with great freedom, with some things changed completely. Yet the central characters, indeed most of the characters, are very much Chekhov's own—and I hope what's finally come out is the story that was hidden in the background before.[30]

Michael Coveney remarked that the translation achieved "an exact balance between ludicrous moralizing (questions of Life and Death, where are we going and so on, are played for rich laughter), physical explosion and that familiar Chekhovian tapestry of misunderstandings, sudden tears and stifled hopes."[31] The reviewer for the *New York Times* called it "one of those rare adaptations that is faithful to the spirit, if not the letter of the original. The play draws strength from the dual authorship—the young Chekhov's ebullience and incipient sensibility, combined with Mr. Frayn's knowledge of dramaturgy."[32]

Another more adaptive translation came in 1995 when Frayn was asked to adapt the libretto for Jacques Offenbach's *La Belle Hélène* for the English National Opera. Frayn took the text in a postmodernist direction. First, he altered it into *La Belle Vivette* and made it, not an operetta about Helen of Troy, but an operetta, set in a theater, about *making* an operetta about Helen of Troy. This self-referential move was combined with the addition of English-language subtitles that not only translate the operas sung in the play-within-a-play structure but at one point become independent and begin commenting on the characters. According to Paul Taylor's explanation, Frayn decided he "finds the dialogue scenes 'leaden,' lacking in conflict . . . and full of moth-eaten allusions to contemporary [i.e., mid-nineteenth-century Paris] allusions."[33] A change like this is always vulnerable to accusations of philistinism, and Frayn was so accused. Writing in the *Observer,* Andrew Porter declared that Frayn "reduces Offenbach's classical figures to Chippendales and Paris to plaster," and he denounced the "intellectual, audience-bashing, philistine level of the show." In the *Guardian,* Michael Billington provided a mixed reaction, calling it "a fitfully amusing boulevard romp." In the *Sunday Times,* Hugh Canning called the adaptation "Michael Frayn's pointless and unfunny new book for Offenbach's immortal operetta," while one week earlier in the same newspaper, Stephen Pettit had characterized it much more favorably, noting that the operetta, "Michael Frayn's crisp adaptation of Offenbach's comedy *La belle Hélène,* updates the vaguely classical setting of the original to Offenbach's own times."[34] But generally *La Belle Vivette* is not one of Frayn's well-received translations.

Television scripts

Aside from his televison plays, Michael Frayn's work for the medium has consisted mostly of documentaries: *Imagine a City Called Berlin* (1975), *Vienna—The Mask of Gold* (1977), *Three Streets in the Country* (1979), *The Long Straight* (1980), *Jerusalem* (1984), *Prague—The Magic Lantern* (1993), and *Budapest: Written in Water* (1996). Dennis Marks, who as director collaborated with Frayn on all of these, calls the series "cultural-historical travelogues, or travelogues with attitude."[35] Producer Paul Neuberg praises Frayn's work as on-camera presenter: "Michael is entirely at the service of the subject rather than busy with himself. . . . He subordinates himself to the subject, so the subject becomes interesting as opposed to him."[36] Typically self-effacing, Frayn gives this explanation of his success in the role: "I turn up shaved and sober to do my piece to camera in the morning."[37]

Intrigue

In 2000, while Frayn's play *Copenhagen* was triumphantly running in London, coauthor David Burke and Frayn published *Celia's Secret: An Investigation.* In 2001 it appeared in the

United States as *The Copenhagen Papers: An Intrigue*. Ostensibly it is a fairly straightforward account of a hoax perpetrated on Frayn by Burke, one of the actors in *Copenhagen*. Writing as Celia Rhys-Evans and pretending to have found some surviving documents from the period when the Nazi atomic physicists were held in Britain after the German defeat, Burke provides Frayn with enough tantalizing forgeries to whet his desire for more. Frayn is taken in; then, having been tipped off by one of the other actors, he faces a moral choice—how to put an end to the hoax or tell Burke he knows without violating the confidence of the man who tipped him off. It is quite a complicated story, made more interesting by Frayn's analysis of why he fell for it: "It had appealed to my vanity, and it had aroused my hopes of a reward."[38] Not only that, he realizes that the situation in which he finds himself is very much like that of Martin Clay, the main character of the novel he was then writing (*Headlong*), who believes he has discovered a lost Bruegel painting. He thinks, "there is great pleasure in inventing frustrations and humiliations for one's characters; this pleasure turns rather sour, however, when one finds that one is being subjected to those same frustrations and humiliations oneself" (52). The book also offers delights of form; the narration is shared between the two authors in alternating chapters, providing fascinating perspectives; there are two acts, each ending in a celebratory dinner; sharp parallels exist, including those between the actors' roles in the hoax and their roles in Frayn's play.

Perhaps the formal delights are too much. Frayn is, after all, a novelist, and this may be not an investigation or an intrigue, but another fiction. This wrinkle is itself incorporated into the text, when Frayn (or Frayn's narrator, also called Michael Frayn) writes,

Up to now you have assumed that I, at any rate, was telling the truth, and that this was a factual account. You have felt as superior to my ridiculous naïveté as I did to Mrs. Rhys-Evans's. What you're thinking now is that I have been at some pains to remind you of the kind of writing I usually do, which is fiction. . . . Is *this* all a fiction as well? . . . The joke was on you all the time!

No, of course not. I was telling the truth before. It's all fact. Up to the last paragraph. And now it's fact again. (82–83)

Of course, this reassurance could itself be in furtherance of Frayn's hoax on his readers, with the overt discussion of that policy being part of the softening-up campaign (Burke explains that he often told people that his hoaxes were hoaxes but they disbelieved him partly because of his confession). It would be almost impossible to prove that *Celia's Secret* was a hoax without undertaking the kind of research Frayn tells us he did in the grip of Burke's hoax—writing to nonagenarian German physicists, for instance. Most reviewers accepted that the book is what it says it is, a true account by Michael Frayn and David Burke of a successful trick. Others hedged their bets. Robert Winder wrote, "This is the way the whole brief book proceeds: it's a series of trapdoors and false bottoms. Not the least beguiling of its many glittering aspects is that, after a while, we can hardly avoid the suspicion that none of this is true, that Frayn never even wrote a play called *Copenhagen,* that every word in this parable of deceit is contrived."[39] One journalist interviewed the author and concluded that *Celia's Secret* is itself a hoax. "You don't need a literature degree in EngLit to realize that, whatever else it is, *Celia's Secret* is obviously not an account of events that actually happened. The structure is too neat. . . . And the two narrators speak in exactly the same linguistic register."[40] Frayn cooperates with sly smiles and provocative statements like "once you realise you've been hoaxed, everything begins to look suspicious."[41]

Philosophy

In 1974 Frayn published *Constructions,* a book of philosophy. Apparently indebted to Wittgenstein's *Tractatus Logico-Philosophicus,* at least in its form, it consists of numbered paragraphs.[42] Among these are somewhat general ethical, onto-logical, or epistemological observations:

> Perhaps we dream because we cannot stand the solitude of sleep. (¶69)

> To be good is to be better than. (¶71)

> Our reading of the world and our mastery of notations are intimately linked. We read the world in the way that we read a notation—we make sense of it, we place constructions upon it. We see in the way that we speak, by means of selection and simplification. (¶5)

Most of Michael Frayn's readers are undoubtedly more inter-ested in his imaginative writing than in his philosophy; and *Constructions* contains a number of insightful propositions about fiction and drama. For instance:

> Masking and disguise are fundamental not only to the tech-nique of drama but to its substance. Characters in plays mask themselves so that they cannot be recognized. They disguise themselves in order to be taken for someone else. They are confused with twins and doubles. They exchange clothes.

Even without disguise they are taken to be, or have to pass themselves off as being, other than they are. They are required to be one thing for one person, and at the same time another for another. (¶151)

This is an observation that nicely illuminates both farces like *Noises Off* and more serious dramas, particularly *Democracy*. He illuminates his practice as a novelist in comments like these:

The central tradition of literature is not description or historical narrative but storytelling; the creation of a fictitious world. Even where the old stories were about actual events and personages they were embodied in fictions, in parallels with the real world rather than representations of it. The factual possibilities of literature are a late departure. . . . The great pleasure of fiction is that it *is* fiction—another world, set among the world we know, often overlapping with it, often aping it, but essentially not it. (¶206–7)

The real pleasure in writing a novel comes when the characters one has so laboriously put together seem to take on a life of their own, as the phrase goes, and seize control of their destinies. Some authors, I suspect, attribute extravagant violence to their characters in the hope of simulating a spontaneity which refuses to develop. They try to generate independence by force. They hang exotic acts upon them— murder, rape, multiple murder, multiple rape—as if a slave ordered to dress as a tyrant were any less a slave. (¶157)

According to Nicholas Wroe, *Constructions* "met with a rather po-faced response from professional philosophers."[43] It has never been republished; and Frayn, in an essay about choosing good titles, says, "I think I realised even before publication that

I'd picked a dud here, when my own agent referred to it in the course of the same conversation once as *Conceptions* and once as *Contractions*."[44] *Constructions* is a good title, nonetheless, as the central idea of the book is the human urge to make patterns, to make meaning; still, the book is a sidelight alongside Frayn's main career. Hugh Herbert summed up both its modesty and its usefulness:

Comparing *Constructions* with serious philosophy of the kind he studied at Cambridge may seem like placing Patience Strong beside Ezra Pound: it is philosophy in an older, more accessible sense. But it is an illuminating extension of the novels and plays, and it does reveal the core of his argument about the way we each impose order on the chaos all round.[45]

CHAPTER 3

Early Novels

Michael Frayn's early novels illustrate his versatility. His first and third novels, *The Tin Men* and *Towards the End of the Morning,* are topical comedy or satire; the second, *The Russian Interpreter,* is an espionage thriller; the fourth, *A Very Private Life,* a dystopian futuristic tale; and the fifth, *Sweet Dreams,* a vision of the hereafter. In refusing the temptation—if it is a real temptation—to keep writing the same thing over and over, as he pretends to advise, he began his novelistic career as it would continue, with a series of new departures.

Henri Bergson has explained humor as the encrustation of the mechanical on the living. Whether this will do as a general account or not, it is a useful approach to Frayn's first full-length book—excluding collections of columns—*The Tin Men.* Frayn has described it as "something of an interim work between a column and a novel" and "a mixture of pastiche and parody."[1]

It combines in a fictional form his satirical insights on many phenomena of modern life—cybernetics, bureaucracy, even sports—and a series of actions that, through human bumbling and miscommunication, illustrate the classic principles of farce. Rather loose and episodic in construction, it centers on an institution called the William Morris Institute for Automation Research, which, with funding from a grotesque tycoon named Sir Rothermere Vulgurian, is to open an ethics department. As the novel begins, Rothermere learns from his public relations man Sir Prestwick Wining that the queen has agreed to open the ethics institute. The consequences of this decision—after her somewhat circuitous tour through the William Morris Institute —provide the farcical climax of the novel.

From the beginning, Frayn's satire of his targets—some of them the kind of targets quite familiar from his column—is obvious. Rothermere Vulgurian is a television magnate; his first name is that of Lord Rothermere, one of Britain's best-known publishers of tabloid newspapers who was heavily responsible for declining values in the media; and his last name reinforces the evidence of his conversation and behavior—for instance, he "stopped to pick absent-mindedly at the impasto on a Pollock."[2] Similarly broad is Frayn's presentation of public relations. Sir Prestwick was

> knighted for his services to British public relations, services which had consisted of being the only public relations man the knighting authorities could find who was not at that moment actually engaged in any morally offensive activity, since he was in hospital under an anaesthetic. (8–9)

The plot of the novel serves mostly as a device to keep the many characters acting and interacting in such a way as to develop Frayn's comic exploitation of their oddities and weaknesses, and it may be summarized quickly. The employees of the William Morris Institute prepare, in their various ways, for the arrival of the queen. Some want a minimum of fuss, others full panoply; eventually, a ceremony is planned down to the minute and rehearsed, with Nobbs, one of the junior staff, standing in for her majesty. On the appointed day, word comes that the queen is held up, so the staff goes through with the ceremony as planned, with Nobbs opening the wing; among the reactions are, "she didn't look anything like her photographs" and "she looked as if she had a sort of beard to me" (209). Just as the staff is enjoying the relief of tension of having the event over, word arrives that the queen's plane is now in flight and she will soon arrive to open the wing.

The main administrator of the institute is Nunn, who knows nothing of computers and is moved primarily by security-related suspiciousness and his devotion to sports. His suspicions focus on Goldwasser, the head of the newspaper department, and eventually he decides that Goldwasser cannot be permitted to imperil the royal occasion; accordingly, he locks him in the offices. Unfortunately, this means that Goldwasser takes the phone call announcing that the queen will, after all, be arriving soon, and he can do nothing to prepare the others as he is locked away.

Nunn is a rich comic character, spending much of his time "playing games, preparing to play games, washing off the effects of playing games, watching other people play games, talking about playing games, and thinking about talking about playing games" (28). A former Army intelligence officer, he is suspicious of long-haired intellectuals.

Around him is a broad collection of comic types. One of them, Macintosh, is trying to create an ethical robot that can act altruistically, called Samaritan. In an experiment with the machine in a life raft, Samaritan I had indiscriminately sacrificed itself for anything else on the raft, including a quantity of wet seaweed; Samaritan II would sacrifice itself only for something with a larger cranium, but did so by staying on the raft and carrying both to the bottom; Samaritan III could push a simpler organism overboard to save itself, but when it was paired with another Samaritan III, both threw themselves overboard. After an adjustment, each threw the other overboard. Forgetting often that the actors are machines—he thinks, for instance, that the struggle between two Samaritan IIIs is "the essential ethical situation in all its pity and terror" (160)—Macintosh is nevertheless dealing with important philosophical questions. After an observer thinks that one of the Samaritans looks a little sanctimonious, Macintosh insists: "'I don't see why it shouldn't enjoy doing right.' 'But if it's enjoyable it's not self-sacrifice'" (26).

Elsewhere in the institute plans are afoot to automate sports, since, as Macintosh says, "I take it that the main object of organised sports and games is to produce a profusion of statistics?" (54) and the computer can do that efficiently, without any payment to the players or wear and tear on the playing fields. Likewise, bingo calling can be automated, from which it follows that bingo playing can, too, and a computer could be programmed to appreciate cricket results; eventually "the whole world of sport . . . will gradually become an entirely enclosed one, unvisited by any human being except the maintenance engineers. Computers will play. Computers will watch. Computers will comment. Computers will store results, and pit their memories against other computers in sports quiz programmes on the television organised by computers and watched by computers" (57).

Another area ripe for automation, since its activities are repetitive and increasingly mindless, is the publication of newspapers. Goldwasser is celebrated for his invention of UHL, or Unit Headline Language, which allows all the permutations of one-syllable words beloved by headline writers, as in "ROW HOPE MOVE FLOP" or "RACE HATE PLEA MOVE DEAL" (75–76). Elsewhere he calculates that a story headed "Child Told Dress Unsuitable by Teacher" should be programmed to appear every nine days (40). Goldwasser has an advantage over his colleagues who struggle with the limited capacities of computers in an effort to automate areas like ethics and fashion; journalism, he realizes, has already subjected itself to radical simplification.

> It was unnecessary to struggle to programme a computer whose range included writing stories about, say:
> A man at Notting Hill Gate who claims to have reduced teenage delinquency by showing lantern slides about development in puberty;
> An acquittal for a man accused of indecent exposure in a park at Ealing;
> A Gloucester Road man who is unhurt after slipping on a manhole cover outside the Shakespeare Memorial Theatre while *Romeo and Juliet* is being performed;
> An elderly businessman from Maida Vale whose arthritis clears up almost exactly four years after a visit to a strip club.
> All the computer had to write was:
> MAYFAIR MAN IN SEX SHOW MIRACLE. (121)

The richest vein of "pastiche and parody" in *The Tin Men* is associated with the character Rowe, who is in charge of sports but actually spends his time working on a novel. Rowe gives Frayn opportunities for witty observations both about the process of novel writing and, in the form of Rowe's various false starts, about certain contemporary trends in fiction.

On his first appearance, having decided that writing a novel is hard work, he is at work on the jacket copy. Free to write anything he wants, he not only greets himself as "a brilliant new arrival on the literary scene" but characterizes the novel as "uniting the sober density of Robbe-Grillet to the broad comic tradition of P. G. Wodehouse" (19). The unwritten novel quickly morphs from a Graham Greene–style story of a whisky priest to a John Braine–like account of a brash young man on the rise. Soon Rowe is back at work on the author's biography, declaring himself "one of the new polymaths. Journalist, writer, scientist, thinker, actor, soldier, wit, temporary postman—he has been all and more" (38). Frayn's enjoyment of Rowe's confusion about the process—next he is writing the book reviews, complete with naming his novel Book of the Year—shades over into pastiche of certain writers and styles once Rowe has actually begun writing novels. His comic novel, called *Take a Bloke Like Me,* is a brilliant parody of Kingsley Amis, particularly *Take a Girl Like You;* next, with *No Particle Forgot,* Rowe becomes entangled in profuse and detailed description that deadens the action—including the observation that Nina Pleschkov's "elbows, coming at the mid-point of her arms, looked almost like a young boy's" (134). Its successor, *The Skulls of Glass,* includes intertwined relationships reminiscent of those invented by Iris Murdoch: "In a flash he understood what it was that Nina had signaled to him about Nunopolos—that Nunopolos had realised that Anna was scornful of his failure to understand why Nunopolos accepted a third vodka with such transparent resignation" (168–69). Finally he begins a jazz novel, with hepcat style and painful puns.

The parodies of contemporary literary excesses are funny in their own right; it is hardly necessary to link them to automation by the jokily involuted conclusion to the novel, in which the computer Echo IV works away at a blurb, calling itself "a brilliant new arrival on the literary scene" for its first novel—*The Tin Men.*

The Tin Men won the 1966 Somerset Maugham Award, given to a British author under thirty-five for a work of poetry, fiction, or nonfiction. In the following year, Frayn would win the

Hawthornden Prize, which has been given annually since 1919 for Britain's best work of imaginative literature.

Rowe's dramatic vacillations from one sort of novel to another demonstrate his desperate inability to be original. He wants to write a novel, but what he really wants to do is write one that has already been written. Michael Frayn is not, of course, utterly independent of the expectations of genre; the comic novel is one such, and *The Tin Men* represents it well, although in his next book he turned to quite a different model, the spy thriller. While it is still in the comic mode, unlike most of the contemporary fiction growing out of the Cold War (e.g., Ian Fleming's *The Spy Who Loved Me* [1962] or John le Carré's *The Spy Who Came In from the Cold* [1963]), *The Russian Interpreter* (1966) is a more somber work than its predecessor, more a work of realism. It clearly benefits from Frayn's own experiences of having visited the Soviet Union and spent time as a Russian translator. At its heart is another man not quite able to cope, a good man, but ineffectual, in over his head.

Paul Manning will eventually become "the Russian interpreter," but at first he is an English postgraduate student in Moscow, writing a thesis on the administration of public utilities. He begins to learn, from all sorts of people, that his "old friend" Gordon Proctor-Gould is in town and looking for him. When he finally appears, Proctor-Gould insists they were in the same college at Cambridge, though Manning has no memory of him, and whether they really were is one of the details never made clear in this novel. Proctor-Gould is in a poorly explained business that requires him to enlist Russians as interview subjects. From the beginning there is something unconvincing about his account of himself and his activities, but he has a certain charm. What he does not have is any Russian. Soon he has enlisted Manning as his translator.

Meanwhile, Manning has been lured by another person, this one a young and attractive Russian woman named Raissa or Raya. On a bus outing arranged by his faculty at the university, she succeeds in communicating her interest in him. They begin going out together and Manning falls in love. When the two of them dine with Proctor-Gould the evening ends, strangely, with Raya remaining in Proctor-Gould's hotel room and, with that, she has been transferred from Manning to his friend.

Their courtship has several odd features. One is that it is entirely sexless (as was Raya and Manning's); another is that she calmly and incorrigibly steals Proctor-Gould's belongings, including valuable Nescafé, a model of the University of Moscow he received as a gift, and two suitcases of books he brought as gifts for others; the oddest is that since she speaks no English and he speaks no Russian, they require the services of Manning the translator so they can carry on the relationship that eclipsed his own. Not without objection, but rather weakly, he permits himself to continue being used.

This odd *Jules-et-Jim* situation becomes more serious when the two men meet Raya's "friend" Konstantin, who turns out to be the receiver of all Proctor-Gould's stolen things and Raya's lover as well—and even, it is eventually disclosed, her fellow Komsomol member and antiespionage agent. Eventually both Englishmen are arrested. Proctor-Gould, in fact, was what he so often promised he was not, some sort of espionage agent, involved in transferring British royalty payments to Russian authors in the books he carried. Almost everybody, it comes out, is some sort of double agent except Manning. Raya's interest in him, from the beginning, was only a device to get to Proctor-Gould. He has been deceived, used, and betrayed by both of them. This has the makings of a grim outcome, but in fact nothing very bad happens to Paul while he is in custody, aside from difficulty getting a towel; he is never even questioned. Soon he is driven to the airport where, reunited with Proctor-Gould, he is deported.

One of the strengths of this modest novel, unsensational for an espionage thriller, is the way it uses its setting. Moscow is seedy; in an early account the narrator describes Manning crossing a plaza:

> Everything seemed enormous and out-of-scale, like one's finger ballooning beneath one's touch in a fever. Beyond the plaza, in the formal vista of the ornamental gardens, solitary pedestrians moved like Bedouin, separated from one another by Saharas of empty brown flower-bed and drying tarmacadam. They were so small they seemed to be merely an infestation. The authorities should have put human-being powder down and got rid of them.[3]

One of the somber figures in this landscape is the other woman in Manning's life, Katerina, or Katya. Poor, humble, unhappy, Katerina is like a visitant from Dostoevsky's insulted and injured. Formerly a student at the university, she has been expelled for being politically unsound; the expulsion was ordered by Raya and Konstantin. In her conversations with Manning, she offers bitter wisdom:

> Some men are women, and some women are men. You and I are two of the world's natural women. We love people because of what makes them people—their will and their freedom—and we expect to be used ourselves as objects—as the raw material on which the volition of others is exercised. Raya must be a natural man. She uses you. She uses Proctor-Gould. She does it not by strength or command, but by caprice, by taunting you and teasing you. It amounts to the same thing. You both delight in being used. (96–97)

Katya is a Christian and that, as well as her passive endurance of mistreatment, aligns her with figures like Sonya of *Crime and Punishment*.

But there is comedy in *The Russian Interpreter*, too, not of the bright and witty sort that enlivens *The Tin Men*, but often wry and observational and, as often as not, based on either cultural differences or the disparity, noted by Katya, between those who dominate and those who are dominated.

> Proctor-Gould became increasingly preoccupied. In the middle of a rather difficult lunch with some officials of the Moscow public health department he leaned over to Manning and said in a low voice:
>
> "Bolvan."
>
> "What?"
>
> "What does it mean? 'Darling'? 'Sweetheart'?"
>
> "It means 'numbskull.'"
>
> "Ah." (99)

Proctor-Gould is an original and strangely lovable character. There is always something ridiculous about him. On first meeting, "Manning felt that he would have been most at home in one of those conversations which consist in the leisurely exchange of heavy banter, like the desultory dialogue of long-range artillery. There was some sort of ponderous charm about him" (28). When he wishes to impress Raya (little knowing that she is actually in pursuit of him, and much more able and ruthless than he), he sings.

> It was considerably worse than Manning had expected. Proctor-Gould hunted about for each note uncertainly, and did not often find it. Manning looked round at the girl and smiled. She gazed at Proctor-Gould seriously, no doubt baffled by the strange modes of English song. . . .

Proctor-Gould reached the end of his song, and there was a certain amount of polite, baffled clapping. The girl got up and walked away to the other side of the clearing.

"Thank you, thank you," said Proctor-Gould. "Your very generous response encourages me to go on and sing you another very old favourite in England, 'Green Grow the Rashes Oh.'"

A stupid-looking man next to Manning who had been trying for some time to open a bottle of fizzy fruit-juice by thumping it up and down against the ground at last succeeded. The cap exploded off the bottle, and the contents rose into the air like a geyser, then fell as a fine, sticky rain over Manning.

"'I'll sing you one-oh,'" sang Proctor-Gould. (54)

Proctor-Gould is a particularly English comic character, and the novel dramatizes a conflict between English and Russian persons in which the English—liberal, tolerant, not terribly competent, vulnerable to force and ruthlessness—finish a distant second to the more single-minded Russians who, in Katya's terms, are—with the single exception of Katya herself—natural men, while the Englishmen are women.

Ever restless, Frayn returned to the comic novel after writing *The Russian Interpreter*. The observations about linguistic laziness and formulaic newspaper content in *The Tin Men* provide one of the sharpest, perhaps because most knowing, areas of comedy. In *Towards the End of the Morning* (1967) Frayn wrote what journalists regularly identify as the best comic novel about the newspaper industry. Ian Johns calls it "every journalist's second favourite novel after *Scoop*," and Jane Cornwell, in 2002, writes that many British journalists still happily quote it.[4] In her *Twentieth Century Classics*, Margaret Drabble also invokes Evelyn Waugh, identifying *Towards the End of the Morning* as "a Fleet Street comedy which can stand comparison with Waugh's classic, *Scoop:* It catches with deprecating accurately the shabby, muddled, well-meaning venal world of journalism. . . . It's a period piece, which ends, ominously, as its characters scramble for better paid jobs—in television."[5] Because of his history with that newspaper, Frayn is often accused of having written an expose of the *Manchester Guardian,* or perhaps the *Observer,* both of which he denies. It is more accurate to say that he has written an account of what newspaper life was like when there were still many national dailies in London, when most of them were written, edited, and printed near Fleet Street, when newspaper unions still exercised great power (and, inevitably, permitted some charmingly slack work habits): before the rise of Rupert Murdoch.

The book illustrates many of Frayn's foremost strengths. It is a comedy, with elements of farce, and is very entertaining. Its main characters are relatively ineffectual, sometimes hapless, average men coping as best they can with a world they cannot master. And it is very astute in its commentary on the world of work. Michael Frayn has always been interested in what jobs are like, how people get through their days at work. This is a surprisingly uncommon topic for fiction to explore—with certain exceptions like English professors, writers, and politicians—and some of his books explore other interests, of course, but here we see his curiosity about, and patient fidelity in presenting, what ordinary people do on ordinary days at their jobs.

The major finding is that the journalists in Frayn's book do not do very much. The title seems to refer to the time of day when they begin to arrive at work. During the last hour of the morning, members of the staff "walked with an air of sober

responsibility towards the main entrance, greeted the commis-
sionaire, and vanished upstairs in the lift to telephone their
friends and draw their expenses before going out again to have
lunch."[6] The main focus of the book is on a small office presided
over by John Dyson, who seems to be in charge of the newspaper's least important features—"The Country Day by Day,"
crossword puzzles, "In Years Gone By." He has a staff of two.
One of them, Old Eddy Moulton, is a superannuated relic who
does nothing at all and, in the course of events, dies at his desk
without anyone noticing for an embarrassingly long time. The
other staffer, Bob, is a dreamer of twenty-nine; he does even less
work than Dyson, who usually forgives him his evasions. For
instance, as the novel begins, he is staring out the window and
eating toffees; when Dyson asks him to make a telephone call,
he responds, "I'm a bit tied up at the moment, John. . . . Got
some writing to do in a minute" (5). After a long lunch at the
pub, the staff return and "by three o'clock a certain amount of
writing was being done. Bob was writing a book review for the
New Statesman, Dyson a radio-script on oil prospecting for the
schools' programmes" (17).

More striking than the very small amount of work the journalists do—at least for their actual employer—is the fact that
they feel very sorry for themselves and for each other. Dyson
regularly complains of overwork and worries about burnout,
and despite Bob's urbane refusal to do any writing when asked,
Dyson apologizes: "I drive you hard, Bob. I realize that. I make
you work like a dog. He writes like an angel, Jannie! And I
make him work like a dog! . . . I'm a slavedriver and I know it"
(70).

The rather loose plot gathers itself around Dyson and Bob
and their life problems. Dyson's are domestic and professional

both. He and his wife Jannie have bought a house in a bad neighborhood, hoping to catch a wave of gentrification. Despite their optimism, their liberal fondness—or at least their public declarations of fondness—for their West Indian and working-class neighbors, and their encouragement to other middle-class families to buy in SW 23, things get worse rather than better. One of the recurring motifs of the novel is the nocturnal sound of rubbish being thrown over the fence into their garden. Dyson wants to get himself into broadcasting; at one point he is invited to appear on a talk show about multiracial Britain (since he lives in a mixed neighborhood); his nervousness is such that, while contributing nothing substantive to the discussion, he obtrudes himself and a set of newly invented mannerisms and makes a fool of himself. Fortunately hardly anybody watches, his humiliation is almost private, and before long a researcher has phoned him up to acknowledge that "you appear in programmes about race relations from time to time, but you're not one of the usual old gang of faces that everyone's sick of" and to invite him to appear on another (154).

Bob's concerns, meanwhile, are almost entirely domestic. He lives in a flat in the same house as Reg Mounce (photo editor of the newspaper) and his predatory wife, who, he fatalistically acknowledges, "was going to get him finally, he could see that" (82). In addition he has a fiancée, Tessa, a simple girl from the country, whom he doesn't love. He puts her off when possible and, since he only skims her long love-letters, is surprised when she arrives in London to stay with him.

The arrival of a new man, Erskine Morris, to replace the dead Old Eddy Moulton, is a new instance of the distinction voiced by Katya in *The Russian Interpreter* between natural men and natural women, or those who get their way through forcefulness and those who allow themselves to be exploited. Just down from Oxford, with a youthful wardrobe and a vaguely American set of mannerisms, Morris is cruelly efficient. In a few days, by the expedient of simply buckling down and working, he writes enough "In Years Gone By" columns to last for years. Told that obtaining a second typewriter for the office would be impossible, he just goes out and buys one during the lunch hour. He writes hard-bitten plays. He composes pop songs, performed on television by beautiful girls whom he brings to Bob's flat. He modestly admits that he has written some leaders (main editorials) during his spare time. When Dyson cannot return in time from a freebie trip to the Middle East, and Bob prepares to stand in for him on the television show about race, both are bypassed by Erskine Morris. And here, too, he is accomplished: they watch as he appears on screen, "talking about certain social developments he had noticed in the Western Region of Nigeria when he had been out there earlier in the year" (246).

It is tempting to say that Frayn shows the best lacking all conviction while the worst are full of passionate intensity, but it would be inaccurate. Morris is not really the worst: people dislike him, it is true, but this is because he makes no effort to get along, because he gets things done rather than complaining of the overwhelming obstacles to doing so and because of envy. Nor is his intensity particularly passionate. He is intensely ambitious. His competence seems unnatural in the context of amiable amateurishness that otherwise characterizes the newspaper's staff.

Towards the End of the Morning contains scenes of the kind of farce Frayn always does well. In one of them, Bob seeks to keep his housecleaner from finding out that Tessa is living with him; trying to hide her underwear, he sends Tessa off to the bathroom while Mrs. Hennessy cleans the room; Mrs. Mounce turns up to add to the confusion. Mrs. Hennessy finally departs, with an imperturbable "You get something on before you catch your death, dear" to Tessa. "If you're looking for your undies, I've folded them up and put them on top of the TV for you. Ta-ta, loves. Have a lovely time" (144). Dyson's failed junket to the Persian Gulf is another situation with spiraling farcical elements, as the charter flight operator fails to get the plane in the air, then flies to everywhere but the destination, seeking new equipment, trying to make connections with further planeloads of reporters from other nations, and buying the journalists drinks to keep them relatively quiet. Eventually Dyson ends up in Ljubljana (this is why he cannot make the television appearance on which Erskine effortlessly eclipses him).

When it was published in the United States, the novel was renamed *Against Entropy.* This alludes to a reflection of Dyson's: "God really was seeping in this morning from every direction, and chiefly through the condition of marriage itself. That was what was holy about holy matrimony, he realized suddenly; it was just another divine instrument for increasing entropy, like damp and coronary thrombosis and woodworm" (135). Entropy stands for all the little things that go wrong, misunderstandings, frustrations, and perturbations. The novel ends on a dying fall, with another of them. Jannie Dyson has been troubled by a woman with an imperious accent phoning to ask for Miss Pennycuick. Having insisted no such person exists, Jannie thinks, "the chaos and fragmentation of life! . . . what about the wrong numbers, and the garbage collecting in the garden, and the slates falling off the roof? . . . Life was all thumbs, she thought, a long series of wrong numbers" (232). At the television center, where most of the cast of characters has drawn together in order to watch (as it turns out) Erskine Morris's impressive performance on *New Perspectives,* the stubborn old woman from the telephone arrives in person and proves to be Tessa's mother: the Dysons have never known her last name. In a demonstration of more entropy—things falling apart, mild anarchy being loosed upon the world, the last word belongs to Erskine Morris, who looks impassively at them all and says "oh, sure, sure" (248).

In *A Very Private Life* (1968), Frayn turned to yet another kind of novel, this one a portrayal of a chilly futuristic dystopia. It presents a strange world, and the estrangement begins with the first sentence of the book: "Once upon a time there will be a little girl called Uncumber."[7] Familiar—"once upon a time"— and surprising—"there *will be*"—at once, this opening puts the reader on guard, as does the little girl's name. Uncumber is a saint's name; a Portuguese woman who wished to avoid marriage to the King of Sicily, she grew a beard and was crucified. She is the patron saint of women who want to free, or unencumber, themselves from their husbands. Other characters in *A Very Private Life* bear names either of lesser-known saints— Pherbutha, Expeditus, Dympna, Frideswide—or Anglo-Saxon kings and scholars—Offa, Aelfric—or even a major heretic, Pelagius. All these people belong to the "inside classes." That is, in a future world made almost uninhabitable by pollution and air shortages, they occupy self-contained dwellings with everything sent in through pipes. They communicate with the outside world by three-dimensional holovision; this, too, is how they visit with their friends. Occasionally there is actual physical exchange, as when Uncumber's parents send away the materials for a new little brother and receive their son Sulpice back through the delivery tube.

Like other dystopias, Frayn's includes an explanation of how the world got to its condition: when Uncumber's father wishes to lessen her dissatisfaction with everything, he tells her how lucky she is not to have been born back in the days when people had to go outside to do things, ate in crowds, got rained on and burned by the sun, and infected each other with diseases; worse, they killed themselves in their "traveling houses."

> They lived like animals; they behaved like animals. There was anarchy! But the reaction to anarchy was even worse. The most stringent order had to be imposed upon people, just so that they could survive their proximity. Society had to be arranged in strict hierarchical patterns, with powerful controls and sanctions. So that, when people looked into the future, all they could foresee was the necessity for stricter and stricter social order, imposed by ever more powerful central authorities, through ever more far-reaching-controls. One day, they feared, every aspect of human behaviour would be controlled by some central authority. Nothing would be private, not even people's thoughts. The whole of life would become public and communal. Freedom would vanish entirely. (30)

In its major details, this describes the dystopias envisioned by Zamyatin (*We*), Huxley (*Brave New World*), and Orwell (*1984*). But

> what in fact happened was exactly the opposite. *Everything* became private. People recognized the corruption of indiscriminate human contact, and one by one they withdrew from it. Whoever could afford it built a wall around himself and his family to keep out society and its demands. Gradually, as people's technological skills improved, the walls they built became more and more impenetrable. (30–31)

He goes on to explain that after the outer defenses against other people were up, people constructed inner defenses against uncertainty and other bad feelings—pharmaceutical ones, the calmants that Uncumber resists taking. To preserve sexual modesty they wear dark glasses all the time though they go naked. To Uncumber's question, "What about the outside people? . . . How are they perfectly free, if they're outside this controlled environment?" her father sputters, "They're not the same as us at all. They're entirely different" (32).

This situation is now ripe for disruption from Uncumber's dissatisfaction. One day she gets outside the house but is rescued by the "Kind People," a police force. Another day she "meets a man" (43). She does so in the only way possible to her: a flaw in the electronic communication system. Trying to tune in a botany lesson, she gets instead a small, wiry man speaking an unknown language. They exchange numbers before the man— who she decides is called Noli—disappears from her screen, and, investigating the number, she discovers the distant part of the world in which he lives.

Her romantic projections onto Noli (at no point does either of them understand anything the other has said) lead finally to an escape; she goes outside, travels by traveling house and then rocket, to a faraway place where she does find Noli. She also finds his wives and children, an ugly world ruined by pollution and the "papooms" (rockets); a place where privacy is unheard of and the contact of other human beings is incessant, noisy and noisome. She becomes ill and recovers; finally has sex with Noli, not very enjoyably; observes him as he beats one of his wives, then sleeps with her; marvels at his baldness (a condition for some reason unknown among the inside classes) and his smelly feet. This, *this*, she realizes, is *real life*. When, having had enough of it, she tries to go back, that proves harder than coming; she spends time in the jungle, sometimes with guerrillas who speak French and kill insiders; eventually arrested, she is sent to live inside but not with her family, dies in the explosion of her house and, after being brought back to life (a common event), is reunited with her family, though only through holovision.

Her adventures seem designed to pursue two thematic tracks. One of these includes some of the themes one would expect for a futuristic dystopia. An American paperback version of *A Very Private Life*, published by Dell with a cover illustration emphasizing Uncumber's naked encounter with a surprisingly handsome Noli, declares on the cover: "The most chilling novel of future Earth since *Brave New World*." Some of Frayn's ideas about the future do resemble some of Huxley's, including the fact that citizens use medication to avoid unhappiness. Where Huxley's characters have soma, Frayn's take Hilarin and Imaginin. Resistance to the use of calmants is a sign of maladjustment.

Huxley's citizens avoid all signs of aging until suddenly dying and being cremated; Frayn's do even better. In an early conversation with her mother, Uncumber is told that "sometimes" you die when you get old, but then "you take some special medicine, and you get better again" (9). You can really, *really* die and be expelled through the waste tube, but that won't happen for hundreds and hundreds of years. Uncumber does die in the explosion, but she is restored to life. During the time that she is on the outside and experiencing reintegration and rehabilitation—about twenty years—conditions change. Upon her return,

Nowadays people are tending to give up having children altogether to stake their little claim upon immortality simply by living forever instead. It was the tyranny of the parent-child and child-parent relationships which dominated society in the past and which so intolerably violated the privacy of child and parent alike. Now that this last old, rusty lock has been forced, the shackles of blood relationships of every sort are beginning to fall away. (152)

Perhaps Frayn's most interesting idea of how future people will live consists in their isolation in self-contained houses connected only by services that provide food, new babies, air, information, and other necessaries of life. Their human interaction has been reduced to the operations of an electronic nexus. Even within the home, the family communicates electronically: the parents "will gradually find it more convenient to manifest themselves to their children at the touch of a switch, rather than drag themselves wearily to their feet and come looking for them in the flesh" (21). Aelfric is a "decider"; all day long he settles disputes, again entirely through the holovision. Uncumber and Sulpice are online learners. The twenty-first century world of cell phones and even more crucially the Internet—a world in which workers in adjacent offices are more likely to send each other e-mail than to speak face to face—in many important respects confirms Frayn's prediction of what "will happen."

Beyond the details of science fiction, A Very Private Life also concerns itself with some important philosophical issues, one of which is ethical. As in Brave New World, happiness has largely replaced goodness. The most striking demonstration of this comes when Uncumber is returned to her world after being seized with a band of armed rebels. Omacatl, the decider in her case, reassures her: "It's not a question of anybody's fault, Cumby. No one's suggesting it is. It's just a matter of finding out what led up to your being found on the scene of the unhappiness. . . . We have to know exactly what sort of unhappiness you're suffering from. Then we shall see if we can treat it" (144). Even after the news that she will be sent off for rehabilitation, the decider tells her, "We don't think in terms of *guilt* and *innocence*. We just ask: are you happy, or are you unhappy, so far as the evidence indicates?" (149).

The larger philosophical inquiry is epistemological and ontological. In an important sense, the inside people are involved in a mass solipsism. Sulpice tells Cumby about his sex life with Nanto-Suleta—in which "they turn on their holovision and lie for hours beside each other's manifestation" (38)—making it sound wonderful, comparing it to being in the mountains, soaring like an eagle, and so on.

> Uncumber looks at him irritably.
>
> "You got all those ideas out of books and off the holiday manifestations," she complains. "How could you possibly know what mountains are really like?"
>
> "That doesn't make the experience any the less valid," says Sulpice calmly.
>
> "It's all just inside your head."
>
> "Of course! That's where the world is centred, Cumby, inside your head!" (41–42)

Reflecting back on her own "holidays"—manifestations via holovision—Cumby is embarrassed to think she used to believe in them: "Only a child would be taken in by such obvious fictions, of course. But what about all the other manifestations of the outside world which even adults accept as true? How can you believe in anything you see? For all anyone knows, it is all simulated somewhere, just like the holiday scenes" (34). This is the same idea that underlies *The Matrix* and other more recent attempts to call into questions the distinction between what is real and illusory—as well as, in a different way, Plato's *Republic.*

In *Constructions,* Frayn wrote: "What keeps our attention in stories is wanting to know what happens next. Odd, then, that almost all novels have been written in the past tense. (The occasional use of the present, one can't help feeling, is a dramatic extension, a device which gains most of its force from the main tradition.)"[8] Even more forceful because of its rarity is the use of the future tense. Passages like these in *A Very Private Life* are designed to defamiliarize: "For this will be in the good new days a long, long while ahead, and it will be like that in people's houses then" (5). Of course, as David Lodge commented, "it is only superficially paradoxical that most novels about the future are narrated in the past tense. Michael Frayn's *A Very Private Life* (1968) starts in the future tense . . . but he can't keep it up for long, and soon shifts into the present tense."[9] Linguistic variety like this is a way of announcing and calling attention to futurity; having served its purpose, it gives way to a less stressful way of telling the story.

In *Sweet Dreams* (1973), Frayn returned to what might be called "genre fiction," though the genre to which this novel belongs is somewhat indistinct and not well populated. The novel provides a picture of heaven (Julian Barnes's *A History of the World in 10½ Chapters* is another member of this small genre). It opens with a man named Howard Baker in his car at a traffic light; he ponders several questions that prevent his noticing that the light is now green, until, when it turns red, he drives on, looking curiously at a girl on the pavement. The narrator provides the result by indirection. He's been unsure which road he is about to enter:

The problem of lunch he doesn't resolve, nor whether to kiss Rose, nor the question of internal trim in public housing. But he does find out whether it's Hornsey Lane on the other side of Highgate Hill (or Highgate West Hill).

It's not. It's a ten-lane expressway, on a warm midsummer evening, with the sky clearing after a day of rain.

The expressway! Of course! How obvious everything is when once it's happened.[10]

The expressway takes Howard to the heavenly city. A proliferation of strange details on the way to the great metropolis—pagodas, windmills, châteaus, unusual neon signs—continues to make Howard's drive strange, though he is unsurprised by them.

In the forecourt of a pancake house the gigantic figure of a woman revolves on top of a pylon, picked out by spotlights, standing on tiptoe, high-kicking. He cranes to catch sight of her face, and as she turns towards him he sees that it is St Julian of Norwich. "And all shall be well," she tells him softly, over the car radio, "and all manner of things shall be well."

He knows that she is right; all manner of things *will* be well in this city he is entering. (3)

The author who undertakes to write an account of Heaven has to imagine what it will be like, despite the millennia of speculation already on record. Frayn's vision of Heaven is different from the earthly life Howard has lived, but not very much. Going to Heaven, he finds, is a combination of becoming better than one was—he can now speak Italian, though he thinks he's speaking Spanish, he sleeps better and is better dressed, he can be a different age at will, and when he regrets saying something he can erase it and replace it with something better—and being a tourist. Heaven contains interesting architectural features, but more than any other earthly place it seems to resemble New York. On the other hand, and at the same time, it is the Platonic realm of ideas, or forms: its museums contain the "originals" of all the world's paintings. "Howard never realised—up to now—he has seen only copies of the Night Watch and the Birth of Venus"; in fact, it contains the original of everything on earth "from electron microscopes and tinopeners to the muddle of Plasticine, string, and electric flex in the toy-drawer at home" (14).

Howard finds himself in a group of vaguely progressive middle-class social improvers, well-meaning liberals like David, the architect of improved housing for the working classes that Frayn will create for his 1984 play, *Benefactors*. One of them is inventing man; another is working on the laws of logic; another is designing a trademark for the Alps; and Howard becomes involved in planning the New Jerusalem. His ideas are muddled enough:

> "So what I think we've got to do," says Howard, "is to set up a society where everyone has enough sort of . . . contentment . . . to be sort of contented, but not so much that they can't see that all this sort of contentment is sort of blinding them to the possibility of becoming sort of *more* contented in a sort of kind of deeper sort of . . . " (117)

Later, in rebellion against his role in planning and administering an unjust universe, having quit his job and moved his family to the country, he imagines the universe that the people will create, once they have made a revolution and thrown off people like "Phil Schaffer, Roy Chase, Himself [God], and the rest of them": it includes both "ice warm enough to warm the hands on" and "bacteria the size of hamsters, living peaceably in the imaginatively landscaped enclosures at the zoo," as well as more meaningful improvements:

> No more excuses for death.
>
> Each man will decide for himself how many arms and legs he wants, and whether he wants white skin or black skin, or whether he'd prefer to be covered in furnishing fabric or mink.
>
> A people's world, and a people's people. (135)

In time, Howard discovers that one of his friends, Freddie, whom he admired at Cambridge, is in fact God. Speaking with the kind of modest indirection associated with the Royal Family, Freddie explains:

> "One can't go writing letters to the papers, like you. The more one can do, the more careful one has to be not to go and do it. One has to think twice before one orders a cup of coffee, in case one's making use of one's position. One ends up pretty much as a signature on cheques."
>
> "But . . ." says Howard.
>
> "To get anything done at all," says Freddie, "one has to move in tremendously mysterious ways." (153)

Nicholas Tucker writes that "writing at any length about Heaven is usually difficult unless the intention is satire, as in Michael Frayn's *Sweet Dreams*."[11] There is some disagreement on what satiric point Frayn is making, or what target he has in his sights. Journalist George Hill sums up the novel as "a concise and mordant fantasy in which Heaven is eventually revealed as something more strictly identifiable as Hell," while for some other readers, the point is how much Heaven is like the world as we know it: Paul Taylor describes Frayn's version of Heaven as "a cross between Cambridge and NW1"—and Cambridge does figure importantly in it.[12] British journalists regularly identify a group of leftish, *bien-pensant,* middle-class intellectuals as "the chattering classes": Heaven, in *Sweet Dreams,* is populated by just such folk.[13] Some readers have seen the novel as simply using the conceit of Heaven to poke fun at them.

It works most powerfully, though, as a demonstration of the limitation on any human idea of happiness. The conventional idea of Heaven is of something perpetual, but Frayn's idea of the elusiveness of human satisfaction works against eternity, and as the novel ends Howard undergoes another road crash very similar to his first one and goes to Heaven—in other words, he moves up a layer or order, with the suggestion that each Heaven is the "world" to a higher Heaven, a meta-heaven, above it. The narrator tells us that, as he again approaches some celestial metropolis, "A restless excitement stirs in him, a sense of being on the verge of deep and different things" (170).

With the completion of *Sweet Dreams,* Michael Frayn turned from fiction to other things. He would not publish another novel until 1990.

CHAPTER 4

Later Novels

After a sixteen-year hiatus in which most of his writing was for the theater, Michael Frayn returned to the novel in 1989 with *The Trick of It*. This new novel was widely praised, not only because his return to fiction was welcome and recognized as overdue, but because the book itself was so intelligent, penetrating, and funny. It marked a departure for him in several ways. For the first time he was writing about being a writer—of course, it is true that most of the characters in *Towards the End of the Morning* are journalists, but that is a different sort of writing and most of them are more inventive in avoiding it than in doing it. *The Trick of It* is centrally about a novelist, called only JL. Another change was much more important, that is, the author's choice of first-person, homodiegetic narration for the first time in his novelistic work. The novelist JL is not the narrator, nor is there an impersonal, heterodiegetic narrator as in Frayn's early novels; instead, the story reaches the reader through the medium of Richard Dunnett, a more than slightly ridiculous academic, who begins as the scholarly commentator on and admirer of the novelist and becomes her husband. He is a professor and this permits considerable satire of the university-novel variety, which, even though Frayn is not himself a professor like many of the more dedicated authors of academic satire, is very accurate and funny through its accuracy. And the narrative procedure is not just first-person, but epistolary. The novel consists of a series of letters from Dunnett to a colleague in Australia.

David Lodge comments on the advantages of such a technique:

> The epistolary novel is a type of first-person narrative, but it has certain special features not found in the more familiar autobiographical mode. Whereas the story of an autobiography is known to the narrator before he starts, letters chronicle an ongoing process. . . . The epistolary novel has two additional advantages [over one written as a journal]. First, you can have more than one correspondent. . . . Secondly, even if you limit yourself, as Frayn does, to one writer, a letter, unlike a journal, is always addressed to a specific addressee, whose anticipated response conditions the discourse, and makes it rhetorically more complex, interesting and obliquely revealing.

Frayn exploits this latter opportunity to particularly good effect. His academic is a comically flawed character, full of vanity, anxiety and paranoia, which he constantly betrays by anticipating or imagining his Australian friend's reactions ("No need for one of your looks, thank you . . . ").[1]

Frayn's return to fiction generated considerable discussion of the reasons for the long break between novels and how it was ended. Paul Taylor, who alludes to the recovery of Frayn's "nerve and flair for novel writing," explains the success of *The Trick of It* and its successors by Frayn's having chosen "tight forms" —for instance, the epistolary convention.[2] The author told an interviewer that ideas had come to him but "they wouldn't work": he had "lost that confident narrative voice."[3] Perhaps his dedication to writing plays during the intervening years—a genre in which his own voice can never be heard and he inhabits the language of others—helps to explain the newly dramatic voice of *The Trick of It*. The narrators of his five earlier novels were not Michael Frayn, of course, and there is considerable difference in tone and feeling between the narrative voices of, say, *Towards the End of the Morning* and *A Very Private Life;* nevertheless, all of those novels have a heterodiegetic narrator— a voice separate from any of the characters—who provides inside views of multiple characters and in several cases manages multiple plot lines. Richard Dunnett provides inside views only of his own consciousness, and does that imperfectly; his inability to penetrate and understand the mind of JL is the most important determinant of the novel.

The novel begins as high comedy, in the promising vein of academic satire. Dunnett is a complicated mixture of professional insecurity and arrogance. The wittiest part of his professional life, as presented by Frayn, is his fraught relations with other scholars who also specialize in JL. He expects that the campus visit he has arranged, at the beginning of the novel, will give him an advantage over his rivals.

> I don't know why I call them rivals. That's not how I think of them. Fellow-specialists. Comrades in arms. I expect my esteemed colleague Vlad the Impaler is always masterfully sweeping his specimens off on joint family holidays in Tuscany before he puts them into his collection. And I'm sure that creepy little woman from somewhere in Pennsylvania who can't spell heuristic, Dr. Stoff, or Swoff, or whatever she's called, is over here every summer with little jars of home-made arse-salve, weasling her way into dinner. I always thought we in Britain were above such things. Or rather, I never thought anything at all.[4]

Throughout the novel he frets about these rivals—though Stoff, or Swoff, has a different name and a different state of origin each time she crosses his mind.

His nicknaming helps to enliven accounts of departmental life. One of his students is the "Female Foucault from Flixwich"; in the Faculty Dining Room, after JL's talk,

> The Bald Eagle put his head a little on one side as he chewed, and watched her silently with those impassive, predatory eyes. The good Pope John himself beamed and chuckled and raised his hand in blessing. . . . Even the women thought she was wonderful. Or at any rate this is what La Beldam Sans Merci whispered to me over the Returned Trays. (12)

Dunnett, in fact, has a considerable linguistic gift. He comments that the part of the metropolis where JL lives is "one of those bits of London where with any luck you could get mugged by Rastas and vomited over by security brokers within the same block" (44). The two divisions of the British press—that is, the qualities and the tabloids—he calls the litsheets and the titsheets; having named JL a MajWOOT—a "major writer of our time" —he later wonders if she is fading from majwife to minwife (107). There is a certain poignancy in this breeziness when, at his last departmental meeting, the Pope

> was rambling on in his now familiar style to me and BD and Lynn Welsh about outreach to industry and market-led approach to the arts, and I was just thinking, "poor old Lynn—this sounds like the final curtain for her dreadful Theatre and Dynamic for Social Change course," when it suddenly dawned on me that *I* was the one who was being brought in for a respray. (127)

His resignation follows and he soon finds himself in a dreadful teaching position in Abu Dhabi.

More serious than the decline in his academic fortunes is the course of his marriage. Having gone to bed with JL on the night they met, he discovers, first of all, that she seems entirely ordinary. Much is made of the fact that her underwear does not match. Later in London he meets her sons and her ex-husband. When they marry, his disappointment largely arises from the discovery of how little life changes as a result. She lives a private life, retreating to a quiet place to do her writing. More disconcertingly, she begins to take an interest in his family—a family to which he seems indifferent, hardly even noticing his mother's death from cancer, though JL nursed her through it.

Though she is his wife, JL remains mysterious and private to him. Worse, she shows no interest in *his* interest in *her*. She never reads any of the criticism he has devoted to her career. Because of her imperviousness, the reader cannot know confidently what she thinks of Dunnett's critical interest, and this fact distinguishes *The Trick of It* from another treatment of a writer resisting the unwelcome attentions of an academic, William Golding's 1984 *The Paper Men,* but the idea of academic criticism as irrelevant to creativity (even if not a malign interference with it) is evident in the relations between husband and wife. And even worse than her indifference to his criticism, JL resists Dunnett's efforts to "help" her with her writing. This is the moment when his interest changes from being that of an interpreter to a would-be adviser.

He wants her to make her novels more academic, more post-modern:

I'm full of ideas—I'm proposing a whole new section, in fact, in which she steps into the picture herself, as it were, and makes some kind of ironic comment on the sheer number of loose feet and electrocuted domestic pets there are littering these pages. This is what would help our strange little infant with his problem—some sense of detachment, or ironic self-awareness. (108)

Her resistance to his suggestions to "rescue" her book are supported by her agent and publisher, who like everything about it except the ironic appearance of the author—in other words, everything but the part he is responsible for—but, as he insists, "The answer is not to give up but to press on—to provide lots and lots more of what they don't like until they learn to like it" (117).

Dunnett seems to be becoming unhinged, and his anxiety about his rivals escalates. The final step is his decision that writing fiction is not hard: he has discovered "the trick of it."

> I don't see why the great castle of fiction should remain the exclusive preserve of the privileged few. I don't see why it shouldn't be made over to the National Trust, and thrown open to the populace at large. It's a trade, writing, that anyone can learn, not a Masonic mystery. Part of my aim is to demonstrate that any bloody fool can do it. (142)

This is a delicate stage of Frayn's novel. He has established Dunnett as a good enough writer to fuel one hundred and forty pages of novel so far; he has a gift of phrasing and an ability to evoke character. He can be the *narrator* in a novel. But he cannot write a novel. He hasn't the knack, the trick. Dunnett acknowledges his bafflement:

> I've been watching her for more than four years, and I've seen everything. But the essential bit—the gadget that makes it all work, the crystal, the chip, the formula, the dodge, the wheeze, the scam, the flick of the wrist, the twist of the fingers, the whatever it is—that remains as invisible as the peacocks' tongues at the banquet. (163)

With the novel's final ironic twist—the letters he has been sending throughout *The Trick of It,* which he eventually concludes are the only thing remaining to give his life meaning, have been lost—the decline and fall of Richard Dunnett is accomplished. He has already recognized the darkening tone of his trajectory; in the letter that announces his marriage, he tells his Australian friend, "My weakness for the light ludic touch may even have misled you about the strength of my feelings. I have been a comic novel. I see that now. I do hereby rewrite myself" (78).

The Trick of It is a rich and deep novel, a MajNOOT. At the same time sharply amusing and deeply thoughtful, it turns on several important themes, some of them universal—the nature of marriage, the mystery of art—and others more topical, more literary-critical. Dunnett seems to embody the poststructuralist argument about the death of the author, the academic effort to undermine the primacy of creative work over that of criticism and theory, and the feeling that "serious fiction" needs an ironic and self-referential dimension, and the plot rebukes him comprehensively.

Beyond its thematic incisiveness, the novel is a significant advance by virtue of its narrative technique. Dunnett is a wonderful narrator and Frayn's management of his voice is artful. As Lodge explains, his style

> can also comfortably accommodate selfconsciously literary writing, like, "One of her maddeningly percipient, odd, crabwise heroines may be scuttering bizarrely sideways at the sight of some bumptious young academic's aubergine underpants." If that sentence seems a shade over-written, weighed down with too many adjectives and adverbs, that is all part of Frayn's purpose. The narrator must vividly convey the

comedy of his plight, but he cannot be allowed true eloquence, for that would contradict his inability to master the "trick of it."[5]

To say that beginning to use the first-person narrative technique, by itself, is the secret to Frayn's renewed fiction writing and the end of his novelistic hiatus would be facile (though his own published comments lend some weight to this explanation), but, having produced such a vivid, and vividly characterized narrator in *The Trick of It,* he quickly followed it with an entirely different voice in *A Landing on the Sun* (1991). The opening of the novel soon captures the detached, almost mechanical tone of Brian Jessel, the narrator:

> On the desk in front of me lie two human hands. They are alive, but perfectly still. One of them is sitting, poised like a crab about to scuttle, the fingers steadying a fresh Government-issue folder. The other is holding a grey Government-issue ballpoint above the label on the cover, as motionless as a lizard, waiting to strike down into the space next to the word *Subject.*
>
> These hands, and the crisp white shirtsleeves that lead away from then, are the only signs of me in the room.[6]

After he labels the folder, "a small sound is audible in the room. I recognize it as a sigh, but have no recollection of authorizing its publication" (2).

The strangely impersonal Jessel (who does not, however, remain this remote through the novel) is a midlevel civil servant, given the task of investigating the death, some fifteen years earlier, of another civil servant called Summerchild. The connections between them go beyond their shared status as bureaucrats; they were neighbors, and Jessel used to go out with Summerchild's daughter Millie. In fact, he remembers the time when she told him she would no longer play in the orchestra of which they had both been members, a withdrawal he associates with her father's death that followed soon after. In the course of the novel, he learns what caused this withdrawal.

The immediate stimulus for the inquiry into Summerchild's death is the threat of publicity; a television investigation is underway, as Jessel's superior tells him:

> "It's one of those old chestnuts that crops up from time to time," he said. "All the supposedly mysterious deaths of people connected with defence. Summerchild is usually one of the cases that gets cited. Innocent Civil Servant, apparently no defence involvement, body found on MOD [Ministry of Defence] property." (3)

Jessel's assignment is not precisely a cover-up, but neither is it a serious investigation into Summerchild's death: it is to establish that there is nothing scandalous or espionage-related about the death, in order to fend off possible bad publicity. It turns out that the explanation is much more interesting than anybody has suspected.

As Jessel reads through the Summerchild files, he discovers the existence of something called the "strategy unit." This, it seems, was a special assignment given to Summerchild in the aftermath of a general election. His assignment was an inquiry into *the meaning of happiness.* Jessel soon learns that the strategy unit had its own tiny office, which he explores; then, that Summerfield had co-opted an Oxford philosophy don called Serafin to help him with his inquiries. Serafin, a woman, had a philosophical approach at odds with Summerchild's governmental one; in an early memorandum, she writes,

In fact his very first answer put the concept in an entirely new light for me. "What do *you* understand by the phrase *quality of life?*" I asked him. He said it was something to do with *washing-machines,* which for a start I found deeply puzzling. . . . After a few minutes' silent reflection, however, I saw that the difficulty arose because we had the read the phrase in quite different ways. I had assumed that it meant the characteristic of being alive, livingness, whatever it is that makes life life. Mr Summerchild, however, was evidently feeling his way towards a quite different sense—the idea of some kind of grading system for our experience, of some variable level of satisfactoriness to which life might attain, and which, as he implied, might be enhanced by various practical means. (75–76)

Jessel's further researches establish several things about the strategy unit, particularly after he discovers a cache of untranscribed tape recordings (left after the two had dismissed the secretary assigned to them). First, Summerchild and Serafin fell in love with each other; while she continued to commute from Oxford, he moved into their tiny office/love nest in a Whitehall government building. Jessel becomes an accomplished detective, reading the evidence to discover their deepest secret: that they had taken to climbing out through a small window onto the roof, where they sunbathed, listened to music, and grew tomato plants.

Second, he deepens his understanding of Summerchild. Initially his reaction is astonishment at the unprofessional way he had conducted his life; then comes a growing identification. After a time he thinks, "I might have been forgiven, I think, if I'd found someone else—someone I could talk to from time to time about some subject apart from Timmy and the boiler and the aubrietia by the front gate" (153). (His wife is institutional-ized and he cares for a son with the help of his mother-in-law and an unsatisfactory babysitter.) He uncoils and warms emo-tionally; from the rigid mechanism that the opening pages depict, he develops more and more sympathy and understand-ing of the two lovers making their "landing on the sun," a term that derives from his realization that the rooftop love nest was "their Canaveral . . . their secret launch-site for the Govern-ment's rocket to the sun" (194). As he acknowledges, "I have caught his madness . . . the spores of it have remained alive in his files, like the spores of anthrax in the earth" (161). Frayn employs a distinct grammar to emphasize his identification, as when he thinks of Summerchild's efforts to catch up with Ser-afin when he has been locked out of the office:

> Now Summerchild and I are both Serafin, reaching the bar-rier and finding no one, then running the list of options through our single conjoint head. What are we going to do?
>
> At this point our two Serafins, Summerchild's and mine, diverge. Mine hurries across the concourse, head down in shameful flight, to bury herself in the Bakerloo. Summer-child's phones. Plainly she phones. Surely she phones!
>
> I'm Summerchild, not Jessel, for present purposes, and my Serafin's going to phone. So I wait. (225)

He knows, of course, how it ends: with Summerchild's dead body in a garden near the Admiralty building. Eventually he understands how Summerchild got there, or at least why he was in a position to fall there.

Jessel writes his expected report; the last chapter begins with those same disembodied hands holding the Summerchild file, and the novel ends with this:

I watch as two pink hands shift the Summerchild file to one side and pull forward the one marked "joint CO/Treasury Overview Meeting, Sunningdale." A small familiar sound is audible in the room, issuing from a point about eighteen inches above the hands. A sigh, experience tells me.

Monday, yes. Another week, another file. (249)

The Civil Servant is back in form. The interlude between the two sighs has not only initiated him into the mystery of Summerfield and Serafin, and evoked some philosophizing of his own about happiness ("Micro-happiness, yes; macro-happiness, I think not" [219]); it has unlocked his own emotion—sadness, largely, about his wife, his son, even Millie—from the folder of numbness in which he had filed it. For the narrator of a Michael Frayn novel, Jessel is not witty, seldom funny; sometimes, indeed, humor comes through, mostly as a result of his misunderstanding of the tapes he listens to. He feels incredulous shame at the broken talk about "the bed . . . lie on it . . . our bed," followed by a "sort of regular pulse—shhh . . . shhh . . . shhh . . ." (188–89) before realizing that they are blowing up an airbed. Another time he hears the taped voice of Summerchild say "Honey"; then, oddly, "Celery." "'*Celery?*' I play it again to check. Yes, 'celery.' The originality of this endearment changes my perception of both of them. He becomes wilder and stranger, she taller and crisper . . . 'I thought we could dip it in the honey,' he murmurs. Oh, I see" (176).

A Landing on the Sun is one of Michael Frayn's novels in which his philosophical interests are most clearly visible. Some of them appear in the linguistic form, the examination of terminology, what it means to say something like "quality of life," but the most important qualities are faced more directly in one of Serafin's dictated reflections:

I am at this moment happy. I know this with absolute certainty. I know this *incorrigibly*, whatever happens in the future, whatever retrospective revisions the future imposes upon my understanding of the world. I know it in the same way that philosophers once hoped to show we knew the experience from which we supposedly inferred the world around us.

Here is what happiness is: a sense of perfect fit. It's like holding up honey and saying "Honey." It's like holding up celery and saying "Celery." These things are entirely true. (177–78)

It is hard to imagine a voice less philosopher-like than that which is speaking when the next novel, *Now You Know* (1992), opens:

We done Environment, round the back in Marsham Street. I just been up there taking a look at it, having a bit of a gloat. . . . That story about asbestos dumping—that was ours. Someone rang me—don't know who it was. Then I rang someone. But the right someone at the right time, that's my contribution. And there we was on the nine o'clock, third item in.[7]

This is a demotic, vigorous, uneducated but self-assured voice, very different from Jessel's. What is more, this speaker is a sort of anti-Jessel, a man whose mission in life is to discover those secrets that civil servants like to keep secret. He would be as interested in knowing what precipitated Stephen Summerchild to his death as Jessel's masters would be determined to make sure he did not find out.

As the novel begins, this speaker, Terry Little, and his campaign for transparent government (called OPEN) are interested in a recent scandal being covered up by the authorities: the death of a certain Mr. Hassam, apparently beaten while in the custody of the police, who are answerable to the Home Office. The Home Office is of course issuing bland denials. As it turns out, there *is* something to hide, Hassam's death *was* untoward and somebody is guilty, and Terry will be given the Home Office documents he needs to "do" the offenders, but by that time he will no longer be committed to revealing the secret.

Now You Know was staged as a play in 1995. One reviewer complained about a "self-consciously literary tirade," which he blamed on "the play's parallel existence as a novel."[8] Another, by contrast, writes that the play predates the novel.[9] According to the Frayn's explanation,

> It first presented itself to me as a play, and it was as a play that I wrote it. I wrote many drafts of it, but they didn't work, and I set it aside. Then it came to me that what the story needed was to have access to the private thoughts of each of the characters, and their unspoken thoughts about each other. So I wrote it as a novel, with the events seen through the eyes of each of the eight characters in turn.[10]

Though the novel continues Frayn's new practice of first-person narration inaugurated in *The Trick of It*, it shares the narrating among the characters. The effect is of alternating soliloquies. The most vivid voice is that of Terry, who opens and closes the novel; his striking style provides a contrast with that of the other voices, all of whom belong to the small but very diverse group of OPEN employees or sympathizers. The alternation of the first-person accounts makes the story perspectival, a collection of "versions"; there is no normative version, as there would be in a novel with a single narrator or, in a different way, in a play where shared stage and audience make one set of events the "real" version.

The little group sharing work in the same grubby office includes true believers and others who are just doing a job. There are Shireen, an Asian girl who answers the phone; Kent (white and stammering) and Kevin (black and mischievous) in the mailroom; Jacqui, who despite her semiliteracy does the newsletter; and Liz, in the library. This is another novel, by the way, in which Frayn writes a very plausible account of everyday life in an office. He is both interested in and knowledgeable about what office workers actually do, and in turn makes the mundane interesting to the reader. Outside the office are Roy, OPEN's solicitor, and, most surprising, Hilary Wood, who is initially a Home Office bureaucrat helping to cover up the facts in the Hassam case and Roy's chaste girlfriend. Soon, having fallen under Terry's mysterious but unmistakable spell, she becomes Terry's lover and a new volunteer at OPEN.

The alternation of voices gives different perspectives on the same events, including Terry's seduction of Hilary. Likewise, it permits different views to coexist without one becoming dominant. For instance, at first defending secrecy, Hilary tells Terry: "It's the same for us as for everybody else. . . . I don't know why you can't see that. We *all* have to be free to discuss things frankly in private. We've *all* got to be able to say what we truly think without hurting people's feelings or destroying their reputations" (56). Of course, Hilary is not even sure she believes this, knowing as she does that the secrecy she defends is not in the interests of assuring a healthy exchange of ideas, at least this time, but in protecting those guilty of murdering Hassam.

A much more poetic counterpart comes from the vision Terry shares with Hilary, just before they make love on Jacqui's desk.

His dream of a world of infinite transparency is oddly reminiscent of *A Very Private Life*:

> "You know what it says about heaven in the Bible, Hilary—it's built of gold. You know that—everyone knows that. But what sort of gold? You don't know, Hilary, do you. I'll tell you: gold like unto clear glass. How do I know what is says in the Bible? I know more than you think about a lot of things.
>
> "Gold like unto clear glass. That's the bit they all forget. I'll tell you why they all forget it, Hilary: because they don't understand it. Transparent gold? What's that supposed to be?
>
> "But that's what is says. All the walls of all the houses in heaven—transparent gold. This is how I see it, Hilary: like all those office blocks made of gold reflecting glass, the sort where the people inside can see out, but the people outside can't see in. Only in heaven you can see in as well as out. A golden light in all the rooms. Nothing hidden. Everything visible. . . .
>
> "And if that's the way it's going to be in heaven, why wait? Why not try and make it like that here on earth?" (72–73)

Answering Terry's question is, in a sense, the project of the novel. For starters, there are good reasons why he cannot tell Jacqui (with whom he lives on the weekends more or less like a married man—weeknights he spends at the office) about Hilary, though the disarray on her desk, the crumpling of flyers in the act of love, and the absence of her crispbreads eaten by Hilary in postcoital hunger all provide clues that require more lying to cover up. Likewise he fails to tell Hilary about Jacqui. Neither of them tells Roy what has happened to change Terry's relationship with Hilary. Everybody in the novel has secrets from the others, and the suggestion is that a zone of privacy is part of being human. Maybe in heaven all the walls will be transparent and there will be nothing hidden; but on earth there will be and perhaps, the novel suggests, should be.

The crisis in OPEN comes from Hilary's decision to quit her job with the Home Office after photocopying damaging Hassam documents and delivering them to Terry. Both she and Jacqui, who has seen the packet, wonder why he is slow to publicize them. The novel has opened with him contemplating the Home Office, the bureaucracy he hates, and announcing: "You wait, my old son. One of these days the trumpet will sound, and the walls will come tumbling down, and all manner of things shall stand revealed. Even at Trade and Industry. Even at the Home Office" (3). Yet when he has the weapon that will blow down those walls he withholds its use, since it will put Hilary in danger of imprisonment.

As one would expect, after a generous amount of the sort of farcical action in which Frayn is so accomplished—the kind of action that, at least in literature, ensues when people are trying to keep sexual secrets from each other—all of the important secrets come to light. Hilary violates the understanding, telling Jacqui the truth about her affair with Terry, and explaining:

"Here we are fighting against secret judgments and secret decisions—and all the time we're making secret judgments and decisions ourselves. We've got all kinds of secret understandings that no one every mentions. You and Jacqui, for instance. . . . You said we were making a city where all the houses had walls of golden glass. Transparent gold. Inside the houses people were living all kinds of different lives, with all kinds of different arrangements among themselves. Some very comic arrangements—that's what you said. But nothing hidden. Everything visible." (265–66)

OPEN is opened up and broken up; Jacqui leaves, and with her the money with which, previously unknown to all, she has subsidized the organization; Terry has lost both his women and very likely his campaign, failing as well to bring down the Home Office.

He reflects, with little self-pity, on the wreck of his plans and his love life (while planning to carry on at least the OPEN campaign), and his conclusion is probably correct: "Either I should have been better than I was, or else I should have been worse. Excess of moderation, that's where I went wrong" (281).

This is the classic stance of modern liberalism: the political and social position that risks ineffectuality by trying to see both sides of an issue. Many important contemporary British novelists have devoted works to exploring the liberal position and its failures, when opposed by committed or radical or ruthless opposition: Malcolm Bradbury's *Eating People Is Wrong* (1959) and *The History Man* (1975) are classic examples, and so, in a different way, is Martin Amis's *Money* (1984), whose main character, John Self, despite appearing to be a monster of appetite and self-indulgence, proves excessively moderate and cannot hold his own against the really ruthless. Hilary is not ruthless: she simply gives herself wholeheartedly to a position that is, despite its attractiveness, only a contingent one. (She doesn't really give herself *wholeheartedly* in the end, as Jacqui points out in her response to Hilary's citing of the transparent gold ambition: "So why don't you do it in front of us all? On the desk. Now. Why not?" [266]) Every human being has a realm of privacy and a store of things that nobody else knows. The question of where to draw the line dividing the legitimately private from the world's business is the conundrum Terry and Frayn face in *Now You Know*.

Though Terry Little has spent some time, among his other past experiences (Thames lighterman, prisoner), teaching English, there is a defiantly anti-intellectual tone to his part of *Now You Know.* In Frayn's next novel, *Headlong* (1999), the author turns his attention, and the story-telling, over to an academic. The novel begins with the machinery of academia: page 1 is headed "Aims and Approaches" and what follows, described as a deposition, includes the statement: "If my claim is not accepted by scholars I shall look a fool. If it *is* . . . then I shall be in a worse position."[11] The term "deposition" is out of place, suggesting a legal document, and Martin Clay is an academic who has strayed very far across a boundary into shady or criminal behavior. The novel is his account, framed as his "findings."

It transpires in the present tense. Recall Frayn's comment in *Constructions:* "What keeps our attention in stories is wanting to know what happens next. Odd, then, that almost all novels have been written in the past tense. (The occasional use of the present, one can't help feeling, is a dramatic extension, a device which gains most of its force from the contrast with the main tradition.)"[12] One sort of fiction narrated in the present tense is that which is occurring, and being told, in real time. The telling is simultaneous with, or just slightly after, the events being told. Both *A Landing on the Sun* ("I lower myself through the hatch, suddenly too tired to think" [244]) and *Now You Know* ("He bends me forward over the desk, until my face is resting in a heap of crumpled typescript" [73]) work this way, and the voice narrating in the present tense is that of someone who does not know what will happen next. *The Trick of It,* as an epistolary novel, is not only delivered in the present tense but structurally assured to maintain suspense, "writing to the moment," as Samuel Richardson famously called it in praising his own *Pamela*.

Headlong is different. Clay frames his "deposition" so that the "present" time is at a temporal position after all the events of the novel have already occurred. But he explains,

> I think that the only way I can come at it, the only way I can bear to try, is to give up all attempt at a retrospective account. I shall have to go back in time to the very beginning, and relive what happened as it happened, from one moment to the next, explaining exactly what happened as it happened, from one moment to the next . . . without the distortions of hindsight. (2)

It actually is retrospection, but told as current action. The present-tense narration is another trait, along with the narration as one of a series of first-person soliloquies, that links Frayn's novels to his plays: for drama is always present-tense. (It is not at all clear, by the way, whether this device in *Headlong* creates greater or lesser curiosity for the reader about what will happen next. There may be no connection between suspense, or desire for narrative satisfaction, and the tense of the narrator's verbs.)

Headlong is Michael Frayn's longest novel to date and his most intellectually challenging, which produced some critical dissatisfaction. "The problem," according to Adam Mars-Jones, "is that there is a substantial monograph's worth of art history in the book, and an equivalent volume of narrative required to balance it."[13] Mars-Jones considers the parts of the novel including the art history to be essays rather than narrative, while another reviewer noted "a pantomime of scholarly activity, a breathless relaying of sources and dates," and a third writes that "to follow the arguments closely, the reader would be well advised to have a Brueghel monograph handy."[14] Most review-ers, however, are much more enthusiastic, regularly hailing *Headlong* as a masterpiece; Anita Brookner—an art historian as well as a novelist—calls it "eminently absorbing" and Penelope Lively calls it "brilliant."[15]

Headlong was in due course installed on the six-title short list for the 1999 Booker Prize and was the betting favorite, though it lost out to J. M. Coetzee's *Disgrace*.[16] One writer, the *Jerusalem Post*'s S. T. Meravi, diagnosed the novel's "fatal flaw": fun. "Fun of various sorts clearly abounds in *Head-long*."[17] It is indeed a very artful combination of intellectual exercise—with strongly philosophical explorations of ques-tions of representation, ontology, and epistemology (Martin Clay is a philosopher), serious and detailed history of art and the seventeenth-century Low Countries—all deployed in a plot that produces ingenious farce and high comedy. Penelope Lively's review singled out a striking nexus of the two modes:

> On page 310 of this enthralling novel the narrator, a philoso-pher by trade, is driving a Land Rover and trailer round St James's square. In the trailer is a painting valued at something over £100,000, wrapped in black plastic and smelling of sheep urine. He can't find a parking space long enough to accommodate both vehicles. A few pages earlier, we were deep into a measured disquisition on the iconography of Brueghel's Massacre of the Innocents. Such is Michael Frayn's elegant pacing that both modes are equally absorb-ing—helter-skelter action and reflective discussion.[18]

The novel begins with Martin Clay, his wife Kate, and their baby Tilda heading into the country. The two adults are both academics; during their time in retreat, Kate, an art historian, will work on a standard work of reference on Christian iconography. Martin, obviously flightier, is supposed to be writing a book about the impact of nominalism on Netherlandish art of the fifteenth century. Like Richard Dunnett in *The Trick of It*, Clay feels some rivalry with his wife and is poaching on her territory; having made her uneasy with his plan to write about Netherlandish art, he has worried her more by a fruitless divagation into one particular artist, before deciding "two months later, that the Master of the Embroidered Foliage, far from being underrated, had no virtues that I could now perceive"; it is telling that he refers to this as an "extramarital fling" (14). The retreat to the country cottage is a sort of last resort so he can get back to nominalism and finish the promised book.

But the plan is disrupted immediately on their arrival by a visit from a neighbor, Tony Churt, the main local landowner, who invites them to dinner at his run-down yet stately home, Upwood. Churt has a plan (which comes out only very slowly) to sell some paintings—avoiding payment of the tax he would be liable for and cheating his brother, the real owner of the paintings—and he wants Clay's impression of their value. Almost on a whim, Tony and his wife, Laura, show a painting on a board that they have been using to block the chimney to keep birds from their kitchen, and Martin immediately recognizes it. His comment on this moment is "I first set eyes on it. On my fate. On my triumph and torment and downfall" (41). Though he doesn't reveal his discovery to the reader immediately, he believes it is a missing painting by Bruegel; he likewise keeps his ideas from Kate and, most important, from the Churts. His reaction at the moment is nicely calculated: "'Very nice,' I say politely, laying it down on the table. 'Most attractive. Now, I've got a coat somewhere . . .'" (45). But his mind is racing, and he has decided. "I'm going to have the picture off him. This is my great project. I don't know how I'm going to do it, but do it I shall. On that central point I'm already absolutely clear. . . . I'm going to give him a lesson in the gentlemanly attributes of ruthlessness and style" (47–48).

The spring of Frayn's plot is now coiled and released. With the ruthless logic of great farce, events spiral into further and more refined complication. Clay has to devise a plan to fool Tony Churt, a plan that requires that he pretend to sell another of the paintings to an imaginary Belgian collector, using money that he must borrow, and take the "Bruegel" almost as an afterthought. Clay has to keep going to London to undertake research at the British Library, delving deeper and deeper into Bruegel scholarship, the history of the Spanish Netherlands, and painting values. This requires that he deceive his wife about what he is doing (he fears her honesty and her greater art expertise). Along the way, his interest in the paintings is misconstrued by Tony Churt's wife, Laura, who is ready for an affair—or for helping Clay get the paintings, as that will be another way of retaliating against a despised husband—and Clay must avoid offending Laura, too. Having promised his wife he will do nothing if there's any doubt about the attribution of the Bruegel, he undergoes wide fluctuations of confidence and has to persuade himself that he has gone beyond doubt. He borrows money from the bank, from Kate, and even from Laura. He borrows and wrecks Tony Churt's Land Rover, and the painting burns up.

The function of the art history and Clay's scholarly investigations generally is to fuel his mood swings. One reviewer employed an arresting metaphor to comment on the plot:

There's a statistic used as a measure of excitement in basketball—lead changes, and the more the better. There are no fewer than nine shifts of certainty in "Headlong," moments when Martin reverses his view of the painting, and each is sensational. It is said to be a sign of emotional health that one doesn't experience small tremors as great upheavals. Some days go well, some not so well, but one needn't hurtle from precipice to chasm. Martin, however, has created circumstances where moderation is impossible. The painting either is or is not a Bruegel; it can't be a little bit Bruegel. And Martin either will or will not spirit it away from Tony Churt. This is not scholarship, where anything learned is a positive gain; it is gambling, and Martin keeps raising the stakes until he's betting his professional future, his life savings, his marriage, his family, his happiness. All based on one glance.[19]

Alongside its satisfying complexity of plot, *Headlong* features complexity of character and motivation as well. Tony Churt is a sort of mindless brute, but ends up occasionally seeming to deserve some sympathy, and not at all the dense, easy victim that Martin originally perceives him to be. Kate, by no means as fully developed a character as Martin, nevertheless surprises sometimes, particularly when she shows a willingness to go along with the fraudulent sale. And Martin Clay is simultaneously fool and rogue, deceiver and deceived. He helps out by accusing himself of the sins of which he is guilty. His desperate desire to be persuaded produces some hectic reasoning—having begun to spy allusions to religious persecution in the Netherlands in unexpected pictures:

I suspect that Granvelle smiled, too, in spite of himself, at Dulle Griet, or Mad Meg, a crazy old biddy staggering out of hell with her pinny full of the swag she's looted from its unfortunate inhabitants. I'm sure he didn't suppose for an instant that this had any reference to his nominal boss, Margaret, Duchess of Parma, Governor of the Netherlands, and the hell she ruled over, but he must have speculated what others might think—you know how people's minds work! (301).

At other times he is inconsolably sure he is wrong and lost. The novel is full of ironies, the most excruciating being when, having pretended to admire a worthless smear of a painting in the Churt household, as a diversion from his real interests, he succeeds in having Laura, keen to please him, steal that one for him rather than the Bruegel he really wants. As he reflects, "I'm like the Netherlandish rulers getting their man on to the throne of Spain. I outsmarted everyone, even myself" (366).

The philosophical interests, the depths of art history, even the class-warfare of the novel (the middle-class London academic trying to defeat the caricatured lowbrow country landowner) are all significant features of *Headlong*. Randy Cohen's review touches nicely on another, which is a recurrent strength of Frayn's fiction and nonfiction alike: its analysis of marriage.

> This is not the first time a Frayn protagonist has poached on his wife's profession. In his novel "The Trick of It," a dazzling display of the comedy of frustration, another academic abandons his field, this time attempting to become a novelist like his wife. Frayn's is a curious view of marriage: We love the other for the thing we lack, then we feel resentment over it, then we try to steal it. There's a certain contempt here. If she can do it how hard can it be? I mean, you should see her in the morning before she's brushed her hair and had her coffee; she's not such a great art historian then.[20]

Once Martin Clay has shifted his operations into his wife's field, he begins to see himself and Kate as competitors—so much that, late in the novel, he tells her, when she asks if he has the picture, "I *haven't* got it. I'm not going to get it. I've lost. You've won" (367). It is true, as he observed much earlier, that "Kate was uneasy enough about my sudden pounce sideways out of philosophy into something more like art, or at any rate the philosophy of art, as if I were trespassing on her territory" (14). But she is more forgiving, less competitive, than her husband, and the coda to the novel, entitled "Results and Conclusions," reports in a minor key the reunion of the Clays, Martin's forgiveness by Tony Churt, and a continuing, amicable relationship with Laura Churt. They are, he says, "normalizing." He is left with uncertainty, not just about the disputed Bruegel, but about much more: "I'm wondering what else has slipped through my fingers since that unremarkable day at the beginning of last spring. What else since I was born, for that matter. Do I know for sure the identity or value of any of it?" (393).

In his next novel, *Spies* (2002), Frayn undertook once again to use present-tense, first-person narration of past events, misunderstood by the narrator at the time they unfolded. Compared to *Headlong,* in which Martin Clay tells what happened just the year before, *Spies* features a much greater time gap. Stephen Wheatley, the narrator, seems to exist in a present day about the same as the novel's publication; he identifies himself as an old man. Beyond the frame, which consists of a short introduction and a coda set in the present day, most of the narrative consists of events that occurred during World War II, when Stephen was a young boy. The main story, then, is completely retrospective, told as if it were happening now: "I go on looking at Keith's house."[21]

The distance introduces other complexities into the novel. There are unmistakable confusions and losses of detail as Wheatley remembers what happened fifty years and more earlier, shared in ruminative passages like this one:

Where did the policeman come in the story? We watch him as he pedals slowly up the Close. His appearance has simultaneously justified all our suspicions and overtaken all our efforts, because he's coming to arrest Keith's mother. . . . No, no—that was earlier. . . . I understand now, of course that she [his friend Keith's mother] and Auntie Dee and Mrs. Berrill and the McAfees all lived in dread of policemen and telegraph boys, as everyone did then who had someone in the family away fighting. I've forgotten now what it turned out to be—nothing to do with Uncle Peter, anyway. A complaint about Auntie Dee's blackout, I think. (34–35)

Stephen and his (only) friend, Keith, are in an unusually heightened state of alertness because of the war. They spend their time thinking of schemes that never amount to anything and play exclusively at Keith's house, apparently because Keith's family is socially superior to Stephen's and because Keith is a sort of Tom Sawyer to Stephen's Huckleberry Finn. Keith thinks of plots, and Stephen helps him enact them.

The precipitating event in *Spies* is reminiscent of Martin Clay's almost inadvertent glimpse of the "Bruegel" painting blocking a fireplace: the older Stephen, the book's narrator, has prepared the reader for something sensational, with references to Keith's pronouncing "those six simple words that turned our world inside out" (16); later, he reveals:

The rest of our lives was determined in that one brief moment as the beads clinked against the jug and Keith's mother walked away from us, through the brightness of the morning, over the last of the fallen white blossoms on the red brick path, erect, composed, and invulnerable, and Keith watched her go with the dreamy look in his eye that I remembered from the start of so many of our projects.

"My mother," he said reflectively, almost regretfully, "is a German spy." (36)

The reader is unlikely to believe this even at the beginning, and there is some suggestion that Stephen only partly pretends to believe it because it creates a new project for the boys: spying on Mrs. Hayward. (At other times, it is true that Stephen believes that "we have to defend our homeland from its enemies. I understand now that it will involve frightening difficulties and wrenching conflicts of loyalty" [57], although even here, the portentous phrasing suggests a newsreel or political speech or some other source of vicarious, rather than real, experience.) Stephen and Keith hide in a privet hedge and record her movements in a book; they steal and read her diary; they take an impression of a pad on which she has made a list.

From an adult perspective it is easy to see where the boys go wrong. For instance, in reading Mrs. Hayward's diary, they note that she puts an X by certain dates: "The X, whatever it is, happens once a month. Sometimes it's crossed out and entered a day or two earlier or later" (52–53). (Keith will interpret this as the nights of no moon, when his mother holds clandestine meetings with X.) There are a very few dates with an exclamation point entered next to them, twice on Saturdays and once on a date marked "wedding anniv" (53).

There is no evidence to support the spying theory until one day the boys realize that, when Keith's mother walks down their cul-de-sac, turns onto the main road, and heads for the shops, she somehow disappears before they can scramble out of the hedge and follow her. Usually she has been visiting her sister, "Auntie Dee," who lives on the same street, and is apparently taking letters to the post office. This is a genuine mystery and eventually the boys follow her to a place where she evidently does meet somebody.

Soon Mrs. Hayward realizes that she is being observed, and she makes a confidant of Stephen; his divided loyalties—torn between Mrs. Hayward, a gentle woman who has always been kind to him and with whom he is in a sort of love, and his friend and leader Keith, stoutly resisting treason—are complicated by a new development, the persistent questioning and barging into his hiding hedge of a girl named Barbara Berrill. Stephen and Barbara smoke cigarettes together and talk about sexual matters considerably beyond Stephen's comprehension. Stephen's determination to find out the truth about Mrs. Hayward, his sympathy with her, his growing estrangement from Keith, and his fear of Mr. Hayward (an implacable and terrifyingly self-assured Great War veteran with a bayonet he has used to kill Germans), all lead to a stunning revelation of what is really happening in the Close. He nerves himself to follow her through a dank tunnel at night and inspects the package she has left, as he believes, for her Nazi spy master. To his surprise it contains darned socks. It can hardly surprise a reader that Germans are not involved, though what happens is war-related, and that activities more common than treason and espionage, and common motives like love and fear, drive the surreptitious visits, secret messages, and delivery of socks.

As the wartime plot draws to a close, the adult narrator again raises the question of his earlier self's knowledge:

> Did Stephen understand at last who it was down there in the darkness, when he heard his own name spoken?
>
> I really have no idea, as I try to piece all this together half a century later, whether he understood or not. All I can

remember is the chill that went through him at the sound. All I can feel now is his frozen paralysis as he crouched there with his satchel half on his shoulder, unable to move, to speak, even to think at all. (221)

The mystery of the man beyond the tunnel actually ends disappointingly—that is, Stephen penetrates it, but there is no public acknowledgment of what has been happening. He is forever estranged from Keith, they grow up, families move away. There is one final revelation, quite ironic. Earlier Keith and Stephen had believed that a mysterious group called "the Juice" lived down the road at "Trewinnick," set apart by drawn shades and swarthy faces. Stephen was bewildered, though only mildly, by his father's preference for him to stay in on Friday evenings rather than playing outside. The Wheatley family, readers learn as Stephen fills in fifty years of later details, were Jewish (the Juice) and refugees from Germany; not only that, but his father was a real German spying for the Allies. This helps to account for Stephen's persistent feeling of being an outsider, a feeling that strengthens his hold on his only friend, Keith, and his sadness when Keith turns against him.

Spies, then, is a complex coming-of-age story, in which Stephen—though he is misinformed on many if not all of the main facts he manipulates—does in fact learn deep truths and get a glimpse into adult despair and adult evil. At no point does Stephen know everything for sure—even the narrating Stephen. He asks, "What do I understand? Now? About anything? Even the simplest things in front of my eyes?" (152). Still, he continues,

I'm not sure, now the question's been raised, if I really understand even what it means to *understand* something.

If Stephen understood anything at all about what was going on, then I think it was this:

That he had betrayed Keith's mother's trust and let her down; that he had made things worse in some kind of way; that everything in the world was more complicated than he had supposed; that she was now caught in the same difficulty as he was about knowing what to think and what to do, the same deep unease. (153)

There are many impressive features of this book, beyond passages of penetrating psychological or moral understanding like the one just quoted. One is the evocation of wartime atmosphere. Another is the completely convincing recreation of the boyish mentality and longings of young Stephen Wheatley. The most beautifully captured is the complicated nostalgia of the older Stephen. It begins in the very first page of the novel, with an insistent and evocative smell:

The third week of June, and there it is again: the same almost embarrassingly familiar breath of sweetness that comes every year about this time. I catch it on the warm evening air as I walk past the well-ordered gardens in my quiet street, and for a moment I'm a child again and everything's before me—all the frightening, half-understood promise of life. . . . Another hint of it as the summer breeze stirs, and I know that the place I should like to be off to is my childhood. [His daughter identifies the shrub from which the smell emanates as liguster.] Liguster. . . . And yet it's whispering to me of something secret, of some dark and unsettling thing at the back of my mind, of something I don't quite like to think about. . . . I wake up in the night with the word nagging at me. Liguster

. . .

Finally he looks it up in a dictionary and learns that it is privet:

> Now all kinds of things come back to me. Laughter, for a start. On a summer's day nearly sixty years ago. I've never thought it before, but now there she is again, my friend Keith's mother, in the long-lost green summer shade, her brown eyes sparkling, laughing at something Keith has written. I see why, of course, now that I know what it was, scenting the air all around us. (3–5)

This evocation prepares several things. On the plot level, it provokes Stephen to revisit the old street (and to tell the old story). Thematically, it introduces the hedge in which Stephen and Keith hide to watch his mother (and where later Stephen and Barbara smoke cigarettes and, Barbara tells him, Stephen's brother and her sister go to kiss). Keith takes the hiding place very seriously, so seriously that he posts a sternly misspelled warning: "PRIVET." When Mrs. Hayward visits Stephen there, to warn him gently to stop spying on her, she chuckles over her son's misspelling, "'Very thoughtful of you chaps to put that label on it,' she says, indicating the tile guarding the entrance passageway. 'Privet.' . . . 'Awful smell it's got in summer,' she says. No, she does know. 'But what a lovely hidey-hole it makes!'" (117).

The smell of privet is one of the evocative sensations captured in *Spies*. Another is associated with the word Lamorna. "Privet" is associated with counterespionage; "Lamorna" with romance.

> And now everything has changed once again. The air of the Close each evening is full of birdsong—I've never really noticed it before. Full of birdsong and summer perfumes, full

of strange glimpses and intimations just out of the corner of my eye, of longings and sadnesses and undefined hopes.

It has a name, this sweet disturbance. Its name is Lamorna.

Lamorna. I find the word on my tongue over and over again, saying itself of its own accord. Lamorna is the softness of Barbara Berrill's dress as she leaned across me to look in the trunk. Lamorna is the correct scientific description of the contrast between the bobbly texture of her purse and the smooth shininess of its button. Lamorna is the indoor-fireworks smell of the match, and its two shining reflections in her eyes.

But Lamorna is also the name of the softness in Keith's mother's voice when she called to me through the leaves, wanting my help, and the pleading look I glimpsed for a moment in her eyes before she realized I wasn't alone.

Lamorna. A distant land across the sea, blue on the blue horizon. The sighing of the trees. The name of a song I once heard. (186–87)

Lamorna is also the name of Barbara Berrill's house. As the frame story nears its end, the old Stephen notes that the house is now called No. 6. That change is part of the loss of mystery and romance that the novel evokes so powerfully.

Childhood has not figured much in Michael Frayn's other novels. He has told one interviewer that he had been wanting to write about childhood but had not seen his way to do it. He entered *Spies* via a remark made to him by a childhood friend (with whom his relationship seems to have been like Stephen's and Keith's): "I remembered something he'd said one day about his mother being a German spy. I don't think we pursued this, but now I thought 'What an extremely odd thing to say. What would have happened if we had taken it more seriously?' But all the rest's fiction, although the street's rather like the one I grew up in."[22]

Another sort of writer, of course, would have written a novel in which a boy said that his mother was a German spy and it proved to be true. That would be adventurous in a different way, but it is hard to see how it could have been more adventurous than *Spies,* and it would likely have been less thought-provoking. "I've been thinking about this area for a long time," Frayn told Jane Cornwell. "Of children hitting on something that they think they understand but haven't got quite right. So they modify what they see to fit their ideas, rather than do the rational thing, which is to modify their ideas to fit what they see. Which doesn't only happen to children, of course. It happens to all of us."[23] Or, as he wrote in *Constructions,* "Our reading of the world and our mastery of notations are intimately linked. We read the world in the way that we read a notation—we make sense of it, we place constructions upon it. We see in the way that we speak, by means of selection and simplification."[24] This is how Stephen and Keith read the world, and it is why Stephen's realization that the world is more complicated than he had imagined is a sort of fall into adulthood.

CHAPTER 5

Early Plays

By 1970 Michael Frayn had written and published five novels. In that year his first stage play appeared. The delayed inauguration of a theatrical career, for a man whose greatest successes, at least until nearly the end of the century, were to be plays, has surprised some observers. He has explained it, in part, as a reaction to the failure of *Zounds!*, his Cambridge Footlights revue, to achieve a transfer to London's West End. He told interviewer Michele Field in 1990, "People didn't find it as funny as they should. But people rarely do find things as funny as they should."[1] But in a 2003 interview with Shusha Guppy he sounded less philosophical about *Zounds!*: "After I wrote that unsuccessful revue at Cambridge, I reacted in a sour-grapes way against the theater. A lot of those early columns were mockeries of the theater, about how embarrassing it is to wait for actors to drop their props or forget their lines. I hated the theater. Then very slowly I went back to it."[2]

His first post-graduation scriptwriting, however, was not for the theater at all but for television. In the introduction to the book publication of his first two television plays, he comments on the disappointment of his Cambridge revue and his aversion to the theater for a long time afterward: "I edged back to it only slowly, first with an unsuccessful television series for Granada [a commercial channel of Independent Television, the commercial-funded alternative to the BBC], and then with an even less successful attempt to adapt one of my novels, *The Russian*

Interpreter, for the stage. This I failed even to finish, and these two pieces are really my first plays."[3] *Jamie on a Flying Visit* was broadcast on *The Wednesday Play,* a weekly BBC program of new, often experimental, televison drama, on January 17, 1968. Anton Rodgers starred as Jamie, a man "larger than life" in several respects, both good and bad. He is a wealthy, unmarried socialite; the action grows out of his spur-of-the-moment decision to leave a house party, accompanied by a dim young woman named Poppa whom he has only met that evening, and visit his old Oxford friend and onetime lover, Lois. While Jamie's post-college life is one of ease and fun, Lois has married Ian, a harried teacher, has three sons, and lives in a very small house on a very small budget. As the beginning stage direction announces: "*The running visual theme of the film is the unending contrast between the smallness of the house and the largeness of Jamie—his physical size, and the general expansiveness of his behaviour and character*" (5).

Jamie's largeness includes an outsized recklessness and thoughtlessness. He is first seen roaring up and down suburban streets in his sports car with a sleeping Poppa at his side; when finally he reaches Lois's house, he fills it with his presence. He is entirely good natured, even seeming genuine in his compliments on Lois's family and home. But he is equally inconsiderate, permitting her to wait on him, protracting his promised ten-minute stay all day long and into the night. He and Poppa stay overnight, involving Lois and the furious Ian in complicated movements of bedding and implicating Poppa in some embarrassment as well, since she and Jamie share a bed though they are nearly strangers. In the morning, moving a settee downstairs, he destroys the stairway and breaks his leg, requiring further stay.

Typical of his thoughtlessness, he has left his car blocking Ian's in, then, during the day, trying to drive with his leg in a cast, backs across the road into a light pole and returns the car to the drive, smashing Ian's car in the process. Making himself increasingly at home, he summons friends from far and near who pile into the tiny house, some bringing large dogs with them, and expect Lois and Ian to give them drinks.

The basic situation is that of *The Man Who Came to Dinner*, George Kaufman and Moss Hart's hard-edged 1930s comedy, though unlike its central character Sheridan Whiteside, Jamie knows his hosts and is doing his best to be friendly. Nevertheless, a premise of unwilling hosts enduring comic trouble for a blithe "guest" drives the plot. There are plentiful farcical elements, including physical comedy growing out of the constrained movement of too many people in too little space; Poppa's presence, whose main role is to sunbathe and to give a caricatured upper-class explanation of her nickname; and the repetition of the word "sorry," necessitated by the physical difficulties. The play has a bittersweet ending though; Jamie's visit has given Lois a glimpse of another sort of life. He entertains her with invitations to Libya, Antibes, Villefranche, insisting "I mean, you've got to get away, Lo! Before it's too late! I'm not going to sit here and watch you turn yourself into a wreck—see you become middle-aged before your time!" (47). This plan is as impractical as everything else he has tried, and probably a bit destructive as well; when Jamie departs with the friends he has summoned, calling out to Lois, meaninglessly, "We'll go off for that holiday one of these days, I promise," she stands gazing at the departed cars, turns back toward her house, and, the stage direction says, "*As she closes the door after her she pauses for the briefest of moments, looking the way the cars have gone. The light catches the shining trail of a tear down each cheek. Then she closes the door, leaving the screen dark"* (62).

The play is excellent in its commentary on choices and their limiting effects on life; like many of Frayn's columns, it explores the conditions and frictions of marriage and family life, especially with small children (Lois's boys squabble and make noise throughout the play). Jamie is, as Lois tells him, a fool, but he enjoys a foolish freedom.

The following year Frayn's second Wednesday Play was broadcast on BBC1, on February 12, 1969. Called *Birthday,* it is also constructed around family, though in this case the main characters are two unmarried women sharing a flat in London and the married sister of one of them. Willa, a somewhat cocksure social worker, and her boyfriend Bernie are studiously unhelpful as Liz prepares a Sunday dinner for her sister Jess. Jess lives outside of London, is somewhat older, the mother of several children and pregnant with another. Her reaction to the life lived by Liz and Willa is an unstable combination of disapproval, particularly of Liz's unmarried state, and envy. Like Lois, she realizes the loss of experience that family life has cost her, though her overexcitement, her announcement of eagerness to be taken to a drugs party, and her heavy flirtation with two foreign students in a coffee bar are all crude and comic versions of the more mundane life her sister Liz lives. Liz tells her, "I'm sorry we can't find a happening or an orgy or anything for you. We'll just have to make do with a coffee bar" (97). There *is* a man in Liz's life, though not in a romantic sense. Neil, whom she met at a party and idly asked to call around some time, turns up with flowers, as a gentleman caller, complicating Liz's arrangements for Jess's luncheon. The crisis comes when Jess goes into labor and delivers her baby in Liz's flat. Willa begins to obtrude her entirely theoretical expertise in childbearing, unwelcomed by the experienced Jess; as Jess is dealing with a contraction by reciting poetry and drumming her fingers, Willa shouts to Liz, "Liz! Liz! Liz! There's something wrong with your sister! She's having some kind of fit!" (106). They argue over whether what Jess is feeling is pain or, as Willa insists, just discomfort, and eventually, when the doctor turns up, Jess greets him with "Who the hell are you? If you're another of my sister's brilliant friends who know more about my children and the state of my insides than I do myself, *get out!*" (110).

In the confusion of the new birth, the fact that it is Liz's birthday is forgotten, though she does say wistfully to Neil: "It's ridiculous when you come to think about it. One moment you're a baby. Next moment you're producing a baby in your turn, and then you've been finished with. The system's used you up. It scarcely seems worth being who you are" (124).

Birthday is also, like *Jamie,* farcical; there are misplaced trousers (Bernie's), and crossed purposes (Willa's confidential invitation to Neil, who barely knows Liz and is not much to her liking, to "marry her and settle down and have lots of babies" [121]), and comic repetition, particularly Jess's insistent explanation, to people who don't want to hear it, of how her earlier deliveries went. But, like *Jamie,* it has an undertone of life passing by and inexorable loss.

Reading through Michael Frayn's early journalistic sketches, one is struck not so much by hatred of the theater as by impatience with bad or incompetent theater. One of the best, "Please Keep All Exits Clear," begins by deprecating going to the theater as a way of spending time, but continues—in an effort to analyze why it is so depressing—to point the finger at artificiality:

"the specially facetious stage voices in which the characters are going to speak." Criticism is levied, too, against the audience: "while it is perfectly possible to find a reasonably intelligent and well-behaved audience for a fourth-rate rock-n'-roll film in Friern Barnet, a theatre in the West End of London can usually attract only the severely subnormal."[4]

Why, then, did he go back to it? One answer, of a sort, comes from Frayn's frequent attempts to explain why, at any point, he writes a novel instead of a play or vice versa: in short, that there is no calculation, simply a response to the material and the way it presents itself to his mind. "I don't have much control over what I produce. All I can do is write the stories that come to me. And what a story is, is in part the way of telling it."[5] Yet there was also an external stimulus. He had already written *Jamie on a Flying Visit*. "Then one of the actors said to me he was collecting a series of short plays about the state of marriage, and he needed one more. They were going to be done in the West End and the producer was an American called Alexander Cohen, who had a reputation for doing very difficult works."[6] Frayn became involved in a real-life farcical situation, however, when Cohen (who had put on *The Homecoming*, in which a family of men famously decide to put one son's wife to work as a prostitute, with her inscrutable compliance) rejected Frayn's one-act because in it a young couple change a baby's diaper on stage. Frayn explains the aftermath: "I was so annoyed by this that I wrote another three short plays to make an evening of my own, just to spite Alex Cohen. The play was called *The Two of Us*, and it had universally bad reviews," though in fact it was popular enough to have a six-month run.[7]

The Two of Us (1970) consists of four plays: "Silver and Black," the one originally written for Cohen, about a married couple revisiting, with a baby, the hotel in Venice where they honeymooned; "The New Quixote," about the aftermath of a one-night stand between a woman and a younger man; "Mr. Foot," a brilliantly surreal vignette about a married couple, in which the man's jigging foot becomes a third character; and "Chinamen," involving more characters (though, like the others, it is written for two actors—originally Richard Briers and Lynne Redgrave) and quite a complex plot. The plays strike several notes that are particular strengths of Frayn's writing for whatever medium. One of these is the mundane irritations of family life. He had written funny sketches before on the way ordinary life, assisted by children, complicates the most ordinary effort: in "Hard at Leisure," a newspaper column collected in *On the Outskirts,* for instance, there is an account of his effort to relax and read a book while the baby is napping, with observations like "only connection with mundane reality of everyday Frayn—small piece of banana left over from baby's lunch squashed on sole of leisurewear shoe."[8] In "Silver and Black," the husband and wife find Venice less than romantic with a baby crying and spitting up. There is competition between them to see which of them will change the baby, along with pretended sleep and recrimination:

> WIFE: This is the third time I've been up tonight.
> HUSBAND: It's the third time *I've* been up.
> WIFE: I was up most of last night.
> HUSBAND: Who cleared up the mess in the Doge's Palace?
> WIFE: (*Turning on him indignantly.*) I like that! What about the St. Mark's incident . . . ?[9]

After a reconciliation, encouraged by the sound of someone else making love in the next room (a sound they initially confuse with rocking a baby), they attempt sex themselves, while the wife rocks the baby's cot. The end is romantic and then bathetic:

> WIFE: Do you remember that day right at the end of the honeymoon, when we came back across the Lagoon in the twilight in that man's old motorboat, and the water was absolutely still—all black and silver, black and silver—and we dropped anchor and swam and the water was so warm and dark that you felt you could just let yourself go, and drift down into it forever . . . ? (*She turns and sees that his eyes are shut.*) You're not going to sleep? Are you? (*His head slips a little further sideways.*) I thought we were going to . . . Peter! (*She prods him sharply. There is a momentary pause, and then, in one complete delayed reflex action, he rolls straight out of bed on to his feet, as at the beginning, and heads for where the cot was, his eyes still shut.*)
>
> HUSBAND: (*Inarticulately.*) All right! Just going! Sh! Leave it to me . . . ! (BLACKOUT, *as he once again falls over the chair, and the baby cries.*) (16)

"Mr. Foot" is another exploration of the changes in a marriage. As the play opens, a bossy and humorless man named Geoffrey and his wife, Nibs, are in their sitting room. Geoffrey is in line for a job, in the course of which, he notifies Nibs, someone may want to have a look at her. Nibs constructs a long and increasingly wild interview with an imaginary "Mr. Samuelson," which becomes a commentary on her marriage:

> "What's the matter?" "What? Nothing's the matter." But Mr. Foot thinks something's the matter. Disagrees with some statement in the book, perhaps. No, something I've done.

[. . .] (She sits down again, watching Geoffrey apprehensively.) "Had a good day"—No, no, no, that's wrong! Strike that out of the record! He thinks that's suburban—something we certainly can't afford to be, living as we do in the suburbs. . . . He hasn't been listening. It's Foot who listens, of course. Foot listens, and from time to time submits reports on the situation to headquarters. That's what all that jiggling is—it's Foot tapping out his reports in Morse. They don't take it very seriously up at headquarters. Old Nibs is having one of her muddles again, they think. (48–51)

Another striking feature of this play is Geoffrey's odd use of language; he employs slang words (italicized in the published script) in a way that seems an act of aggression: the investigator who may come around to "take a *decko* at you from close to" won't be easy to recognize: "He'll be disguised as a brush salesman, or a market-research *Johnny*" (43). This may be a comment on class: Geoffrey, though he seems a don, is actually a businessman; talking about sending "a *dick*" round to "*have a squint*" (43), luxuriating in his Australian and hard-bitten-detection terminology, is a sort of verbal violence toward his wife, a brief intermission in his indifference.

"Chinamen" is the longest of the four plays in this collection. In it a couple giving a party are inadvertently hosting a threesome—a married couple, now separated (Bee and Barney), and the wife's new partner, Alex. The evening becomes a frantic effort to keep Barney and Alex from coming face to face. In this two-part play, the actor plays both Barney and Stephen (the host), while the actress plays Stephen's wife Jo, Bee, and Alex, Bee's new love interest, who is "a beardless young man with a great mop of frizzy hair and bell-bottomed trousers, and is hung about with chains and dingle-dangles; almost complete ambiguous as to sex and class" (77). There are multiple near misses, as well as confusions about gender (when Barney glimpses Alex he mistakes him for Jo's *au pair* girl) and language, as in the following dialogue between Barney, who thinks Alex is the girl who takes care of Stephen and Jo's children, and Alex, who runs a discotheque:

> BARNEY: Doesn't it get you down, looking after the children all the time?
>
> ALEX: The kids? No . . . I don't get much trouble. There's the usual business about, you know, pot.
>
> BARNEY: They still use the pot, do they?
>
> ALEX: Oh, yeah, most of them.
>
> BARNEY: That must make a lot of extra work for you.
>
> ALEX: Oh, I just try to stop them getting busted.
>
> BARNEY: The pots?
>
> ALEX: The kids. I mean, you know, I try to sort of keep the fuzz off their necks as much as possible.
>
> BARNEY: That's a problem, is it, the fuzz on their necks?
>
> ALEX: Oh, you get the fuzz round, you know, twice a night, sometimes.
>
> BARNEY: It's funny, Alex—I feel I can talk to you. I feel we somehow understand each other. Do you feel that? (79)

What follows is Barney making a pass at Alex (he is quite drunk and has earlier made a pass at Jo). Barney and Bee compare Barney's wife with "the bird Alex is going round with" (80)—Barney still thinking Alex is a woman, but now a lesbian—finding many points of similarity without ever realizing that they are both discussing Bee. Later, Bee makes a pass at Stephen. All this time there is another couple, John and Laura, who never appear but are spoken to offstage.

In short, with frantic entrances and exits, much talking at cross-purposes, confusions about identity and gender, accelerating falsehoods, and rapid, complex action, "Chinamen" is a farce. This is a genre in which Frayn was to write many successful plays and to which his greatest theatrical success, *Noises Off*, is a brilliant contribution. John Wilders comments that in "Chinamen," as "in a great many farces, much play is made with the doors"—a recognition that hiding and revealing, by means of coming on and off stage, are at the heart of the genre.[10] Katharine Worth refers to the satisfaction provided by the best farces: "allowing disorder such a seemingly free run while maintaining unshakeable order."[11] And Frayn has commented penetratingly on what farce is and how it works.

> Farce has always been regarded in this country, in fact everywhere, as rather downmarket, popular entertainment. . . . When I first started writing farces, interviewers would ask me, "Why do you do farces? Why don't you write about life as it is?" and I couldn't understand what their lives must be like. I mean it seems to be that everyday life has a very strong tendency towards farce, that is to say, things go wrong. And they go wrong often in a very complex and logically constructed way—one disaster leads to another, and the combination of two disasters leads to a third disaster, which is the essence of classical farce: disaster building upon itself. . . . I think what most farces have in common is the element of panic. People lose their heads. They find themselves in an embarrassing situation, and they tell a lie to cover up. The lie doesn't make things better, it makes them worse, and they

then have to explain not only the initial embarrassing situation but the lie as well, and the panic escalates.[12]

These remarks were made mostly about *Noises Off,* Frayn's most famous farce, but they apply just as well to "Chinamen," or to *Clockwise* (the John Cleese film he wrote), or many of his other plays.

But not all of Frayn's plays, even his early ones, are farces (one should remember, and take seriously, his statement that he is unable to follow his own advice, to find a successful formula and cleave to it). His next production, *Alphabetical Order* (1976), though it has frequent entrances and exits, has a less tensely coiled plot than "Chinamen" and lacks the farcical elements of panic, lying and then lying to cover original lies, and steadily rising complication. In this play, set in the clippings library of a provincial newspaper, not very much happens. In act 1, a young woman named Leslie begins work in the library as an assistant to the harried but good-natured Lucy, who is in charge of the chaotic collection. Act 2 shows that Leslie has thoroughly reorganized the library, reducing it to "alphabetical order" and imposing, simultaneously, some repressive rules that make the library a less enjoyable, though presumably more efficient, office. (Leslie is akin to Erskine Morris, the efficient young man whose hiring highlights the amiable inefficiency of the office in *Towards the End of the Morning.*) The telephone will not be answered before 2:00 P.M.; files will be returned immediately to their places rather than staying on tables or the floor as in act 1. The ironic payoff to Leslie's efforts comes when staff members discover that the newspaper has ceased publication and they are all out of work. Their response is a tension-releasing carnival of disorder, flinging the files around the room and destroying the careful order of the library—which is, of course, no longer needed for a newspaper that has ceased to exist. Though Leslie encourages her colleagues to fight back and put out the paper themselves, there is little reason to think this can happen. In fact, the room has returned to a sort of stasis occasionally reminiscent of *Waiting for Godot*. The tone is captured in this conversation between Lucy and her co-worker Wally:

LUCY: Now or never, Wally

WALLY: Sooner or later.

LUCY: Didn't you hear what I said?

WALLY: When the horse is up to it [a reference to a horse-back elopement they repetitively joke about].

LUCY: Go on, then, Wally. Go to the meeting.

WALLY: One of these days.

LUCY: That's right. One of these days.

WALLY: When the revolution comes.

LUCY: That *was* the revolution.

WALLY: One of these days. (*He squeezes her hand.*)

    Wally smiles and goes out. Lucy takes the apple out of her desk, and begins to eat it. CURTAIN[13]

Commenting on the critical reaction to the play, Frayn writes:

I sometimes feel a little ashamed when sympathetic critics try to rescue me from my disgrace by identifying good or bad characters, or right and wrong causes. Some reviewers saw *Alphabetical Order,* for instance, as a polemic against the dangers of soulless efficiency, with Lucy, the untidy senior librarian, as heroine, and with Leslie, her tidy-minded assistant, as villain. . . . It seems ungrateful to disagree, and I suppose my own opinion lacks the objectivity of theirs. But I think *Alphabetical Order* is about the *interdependence* of order and disorder—about how any excess of the one makes you long for the other—about how the very possibility of one implies the existence of the other.[14]

A presentation of disorder—or for that matter, order—does not make a play. What does? There is very little action in *Alphabetical Order*—occasionally people find information, magazines are brought in and distributed preparatory to being ignored or discarded, a few clippings are cut out, the phone rings and Lucy or Leslie provides some information—but the play is mostly dialogue. The character of the discourse is amiable but pointless, with a sort of harmless facetiousness that never rises to anything memorable.

LUCY: Don't take any notice of *him*.
GEOFFREY: Everyone loves our Lucy. I was right, wasn't I?
LESLIE: Yes.
LUCY: Geoffrey is a kind of endurance test we put all our new members of staff through.
GEOFFREY: No, seriously, though, isn't she a smasher?
LUCY: It's like having some huge dog licking your face and knocking everything over with its tail.
GEOFFREY: She is, though, isn't she? Isn't she? Isn't she?
LESLIE: Yes. Great. (17)

The forced bonhomie tends to hide differences among the various staffers—John is a former don with an inconsequential way of speaking, Wally a waggish flirt, Nora an aging widow with designs on Arnold, who is an alcoholic—even when glimpses of more serious matters peer through. Arnold's wife is in the hospital, and Nora wants to take him on, but Lucy does instead. In act 1, John lives with Lucy; in act 2, with Leslie. As Lucy tells Leslie—who has not been amused by all the strenuous facetiousness—"There was this whole venerable organization clowning away for an audience of one. And there was the audience of one gazing coldly back" (33). Leslie's unwillingness to laugh at unfunny remarks intended as jokes, combined with her analytical side—Lucy accuses her of "classifying away. This is a deaf man. This is a drunk" (33)—set her apart from the rest. Of course, classification is a useful skill for a librarian to possess, and Leslie has clearly made the library more usable when, in act 2, she has implemented a classification scheme.

There is a bit of philosophizing among the jokes. Leslie, suggesting that the future of the paper is brighter than the staff members recognize, insists, "You mustn't let yourself be impressed by something you believe in. That's what's wrong with this place. Isn't it?" (33). Earlier she had explained her inability to find the place exciting by remarking, "Things don't have any value in themselves. Do they? It's just what we do with them, what use we make of them" (32). This is as close as the play comes to an open investigation of the philosophical position that Frayn identifies as the theme of his first five plays:

It might be objected that one single theme is somewhat sparse provision to sustain five separate and dissimilar plays. I can only say that it is a theme which has occupied philosophers for over two thousand years, and one which is likely to occupy them for at least two thousand more. In fact it is the theme of philosophy, the central puzzle at the heart of all our speculations upon epistemology and perception, upon free will and determinism, upon the value-systems of ethics and aesthetics, upon the nature of mathematics and God and language; it is the central puzzle of life. The dilemma is this: the world plainly exists independently of us—and yet it equally plainly exists only through our consciousness of it.[15]

Benedict Nightingale sums up *Alphabetical Order* as "a splendidly witty and amusing play, with a melancholy, wistful and at times almost childlike undertow. Wouldn't it be nice if we could spend our adult lives lolling on cabinets, imitating dogs and frogs, meaninglessly flirting with the girls, throwing magazines onto the floor and showers of paper into the air? Isn't a pity that Mummy, or someone like her, always seems to stop us?"[16]

Some viewers, or readers, may be tempted to accredit John, the absent-minded ex-academic, as an authorial representative, because of his interest in philosophy. But it is an unimpressive performance for a philosopher: his contribution to the philosophy of language is this:

> JOHN: With gold I associate words like endomorphic, somatic, meridional, holistic, good digestion. Silver I tend to locate in a cluster which contains ectomorphic, cerebral, nocturnal, analytic, spasm of the colon. Do you suffer from indigestion at all?
>
> LESLIE: No.
>
> JOHN: No, nor do I. I suppose all systems of classification break down at some point. (7)

Again, ponderously chatting up Leslie, he explains:

> You can't help wondering, and when I say you I mean one, and when I say one I mean I, you can't help wondering about the fundamental doctrine of logical atomism that the world is everything which is the case [Proposition I from Wittgenstein's *Tractatus Logico-Philosophicus*]. Because at each moment more and more is the case, so that if the world is everything which is the case, then the world is in a state of continuous expansion, or perhaps, more properly, in a state

of continuously increasing logical density. Logical space, which is the domain of the propositions of language, begins empty, and then, as the universe ages, becomes ever more densely filled with the structure of fact, which may offer a good analogy with the picture which some cosmologists have proposed of the continuous creation of matter in physical space, and which certainly suggests to me, though perhaps not yet to you, a room gradually filling up with dog-eared yellowing newspaper until one can no longer breathe. So why don't you and I say as it were sod all this, and as it were slide off to the flicks for the afternoon? (8)

Leslie pays no attention to this. John has arrived looking for a quotation about competition in education, very approximately remembered and attributed to a Labour party spokesman; at the very end of act 1 the efficient Leslie tracks it down, identifying it as a line from Samuel Johnson. John's reaction is "that's no use, then" (40), in another illustration of the shortcomings of efficiency and getting things done, which (while it also recognizes the shortcomings of *inefficiency,* no matter how charming, and of *not* getting things done) is part of the point of the play.

Frayn's next two plays share a common structural device—a number of men whose competition is fueled by their common attraction to the single woman in each play—but are otherwise very different. *Donkey's Years* (1977) features graduates returning to their college for a twenty-year reunion; *Clouds* (also 1977), three writers on a visit to Cuba. *Donkey's Years* is more easily assignable to the category of farce; *Clouds,* based as it is on a reporting visit Frayn himself made to Cuba and engaging some of the philosophical issues canvassed in *Constructions,* is not without its farcical elements, but its tone is quite different.

Donkey's Years begins in "one of the smaller courts, in one of the lesser colleges, at one of the older universities."[17] Acts 2 and 3 take place in student rooms in the same college. Frayn's own explanation of the play is that

> [in] *Donkey's Years* middle-aged men find themselves con-
> fronted by the perceptions they formed of each other—and of
> themselves—when they were young, and by the styles of
> being they adapted then to give themselves shape in each
> other's eyes, and in their own. In the ensuing years they have
> all, consciously or unconsciously, slipped out of these shells,
> and when for one night they try to re-inhabit them the effect
> is as absurd as wearing outgrown clothes would be.[18]

The expository portion of the play consists of conversations among the returned old boys and between themselves and the college porter, Birkett, still in place after fifty years. Their con-versations reveal their positions in life—one is a government minister, one a priest, one a journalist, and so on; their likes and dislikes, petty point-scorings and adjustments of hierarchy; and the difficulty, experienced by many who have attended reunions, of making meaningful conversation. They tell how many chil-dren they have, and they recall old times (this is how they try to re-inhabit their old shells).

There are two misfits in the group. One is the only woman, Lady Driver, who is the wife of the college master, presiding in his absence. A woman of importance and dignity, she was also, it becomes clear, the object of the affections of many of the men in the college, who recall her arriving on her bicycle in the evening and climbing out of the college building in the morning after an illicit assignation in an undergraduate's room, her dress caught on the spikes of the wall. She has changed, she insists, though several of the men, including a young don currently on staff, try to make assignations with her. She hasn't changed completely, though; it is just that her heart belongs to a certain "Roddy," whom nobody has seen since college and about whom fantastic rumors circulate.

The other misfit, a man called Snell, arrives. Having failed to make any impression as an undergraduate, he is unrecognized by all and fails to impress as an alumnus as well. Because he lived in lodgings distant from the college "out beyond the station" (a phrase that functions here in several contexts as a marker for exclusion), he missed all the fun of the undergraduate years, and in due course, he demands to be admitted now as a mature student so he can drink and party and have women in the college. Because he lived in lodgings when he was an undergraduate, he has no former room to be assigned to and is given the one Roddy will not need because he isn't coming to the reunion. Only he knows that he is using Roddy's old room. When the others arrive there for a party, to which they have invited themselves on the strength of good old Roddy's reputation, they snub and condescend to Snell, not knowing they are his guests; they also, more sensationally, do not know that Lady Driver, having arrived for a reunion with Roddy, is hiding in the bedroom.

From the middle of act 2 through the end of the play, the comic action accelerates: Lady Driver appears dressed in several different suits of clothing, mostly men's; climbing out the window, she is taken for Snell or a potential suicide on the tower. Headingley, the government minister, makes a comic confusion in his attempts to shave and, as the play ends, is spraying shaving cream into his armpit.

As in plays like *Jamie on a Flying Visit* and *Birthday*, *Donkey's Years* is not without some poignancy deriving from the awareness of passing time and missed life. Neither the fact that the "fun" of undergraduate life may have been insubstantial nor the fact that the complaint arises from Snell, the undergraduate nobody who has now become a boring and mentally unbalanced student of parasitology, completely undermines Snell's lament:

> SNELL: I never sat up all night when I was an undergraduate. I never sat up talking all night. I never sat up reading all night. Lock the door, light a pipe, bank up the fire . . . Ha!
>
> . . .
>
> SNELL: And as for having a girl in my rooms all night . . . ! What? Out beyond the station? Don't make me laugh!
>
> HEADINGLEY: See Dr. Taylor.
>
> SNELL: I wasted my time here! That's the tragedy. I wasted three years of my life. I just worked, and worked, and cycled back and forth to my lodgings, and worked and drank Nescafé, and worked, and got a second.
>
> HEADINGLEY: Across the landing.
>
> SNELL: I never wore a fancy waistcoat.
>
> HEADINGLEY: Dr Taylor.
>
> SNELL: I never wrote a blasphemous poem. I never had a bath in a women's college.
>
> HEADINGLEY: Get the forms from Dr Taylor.
>
> SNELL: I wasn't ready for it, you see. That was the thing. I didn't know the trick, I hadn't got the knack. I wasn't old enough to be young. (144)

Clouds, staged in the same year, represents one of Frayn's first experiments in form. Unlike many of the playwrights who came to prominence in the British theater of the 1960s and 1970s, he had not been particularly innovative in the form of his plays, at least until his late plays *Copenhagen* and *Democracy.*

He tends to divide his plays into two or three acts; they take place, usually, on realistic sets; characters have names that do not change during the play; and the language, while of course stylized like all stage dialogue, is comprehensible. His career has left the way plays are staged and performed much as they were when he began playwrighting. And *Clouds* is not a radical departure from traditional stagecraft, except within the context of Frayn's own work. The staging is minimalist; on a stage constructed to offer a choice of levels there are six chairs and a table, which are visibly rearranged between scenes to represent a desk, a dining table, the interior of a Cadillac. Spotlights are used to isolate characters when they are alone, thinking or writing, in parallel. The scenery is a bare sky. The spareness of set liberates the play, in a sense, which presents five characters traveling around Cuba whose travels are represented by having them ride in a car (i.e., sit in the chairs) and comment on the passing scene.

A man and a woman meet on the stage and begin speaking to each other with great care:

MARA: (*Enunciates carefully,*) I am late.

OWEN: (*Likewise.*) I am hot.

MARA: I sit outside.

OWEN: I come in here.

MARA: I close my eyes in the sunlight.

OWEN: I find no one.

MARA: I cannot move.

OWEN: Now I am cool.

MARA: Please forgive me.

OWEN: *Buenos dias.*

MARA: *Buenos dias.*[19]

The conversation continues in this vein for more than a page before they attempt something a bit more daring.

> OWEN: Your country is famous for its beautiful women!
> MARA: Yes?
> OWEN: Yes! Now I see it with my own eyes!
> MARA: People say that the men in your country are very passionate! Is that so?
> OWEN: We have a certain dogged persistence that seems to go down quite well in some quarters. (173)

With that ironic understatement they realize simultaneously that both are English.

After a bit of competitive sniping—they are both English *writers,* commissioned by competing Sunday newspaper magazine supplements—another man enters, speaking Spanish. He proves to be an American, an academic, also covering Cuba. He is knowledgeable and experienced, and committed—an enthusiast for the Cuban revolution. The three end up touring together because there is only one available car.

One source of tension in the group is that each of the men (including Angel, their guide, and Hilberto, their driver) is interested in Mara, and all try various stratagems to achieve an advantage over each other. A more important one is the question of the proper approach to Cuba. It is an epistemological question as well as a professional, procedural one. Angel is an employee of the Cuban government, assigned to produce a positive image. Ed Budge, the American, is an enthusiast. He sees visions: where there seems to be only dusty scaffolding, he insists, "what you're looking at here, Owen, is not dust and emptiness, but ten thousand people and their lives" (203). Mara is a writer of romantic novels. Owen speaks for journalism: "Some people don't understand—reporters are supposed to say what the world's like, not make the world like they say" (201). Ed and Owen clearly frame the epistemological question—the world as real phenomenon versus the world as created by human consciousness of it—identified by Frayn as the theme of his early plays. The opening confusion in which Owen and Mara each constructed an imagined Cuban to talk to and a special English in which to talk is a comic way of raising the same issue. At the beginning of act 2, they are looking up at the clouds and detecting (or is it creating?) pictures there. As Mara outlines what she sees—Owen with his wife and children, somewhat drunk, with a lop-sided smile on his face as he tries to explain something to his wife—the emphasis is clearly on the constitutive power of the human mind.

Interest in Mara eventually produces a fight between Angel and Owen in which Ed, trying to be a peacemaker, is felled with a chair. This scene is played in a series of blackouts. The final one shows a new arrangement—the three in the rear of the car, sulky and injured, while Mara rides up front with Hilberto. Her speech echoes an earlier one by Ed. He had rhapsodized:

> Did you see? A boy walking along a country road. And the sun's shining. And there's no traffic on the road to hassle him. . . . He's chewing a piece of sugar cane. And he's as happy as a mouse in a cracker-barrel! Look at this old feller. . . . Sitting back on his donkey. Hand on hip. Straw hat on his head. Cigar in his mouth. Looking as if he owns the whole damned place. Which he does! That's Cuba back there, riding on that donkey. (183–84)

Now Mara (who had little to say early in the play) is at her ease:

> MARA: Look at that old boy on the donkey! Big cigar! Sitting back, looking as if he owned the place!

HILBERTO: Whee—heeeee!

MARA: And look at this old boy in the Cadillac! Also looking very content with life!

HILBERTO: Whee—heeeee!

MARA: And look at that sky. Not a cloud in sight. Pure
light. Pure emptiness. Everything. (254)

Clouds is stark, economical, and poetic; it was followed by a
more realistic, dense work. In *Make and Break* (1980), Frayn
returned to a more familiar kind of play, though the setting is an
unusual one. A group of English businessmen plus one woman
have gone to Frankfurt for a trade fair; they are in the business
of selling movable partitions. Though there is a display in the
exhibition hall, offstage, the setting of the play is in a hotel suite,
where demonstration units are set up and various English salesmen are working on assorted foreign prospective buyers.
Despite the tightly contained setting of the play, salesmen in a
hotel suite, so different from that of *Clouds,* its action too is
affected by two features of then-contemporary social and political history. There are regular explosions audible during the
play, the distant and not-so-distant evidence of bombs. And all
the Englishmen are driven in part by recession in the United
Kingdom, which is the impetus for their being in Frankfurt trying to sell partitions to Eastern Europeans and Middle Eastern-
ers. That also explains the anxiety over the possible closing
down or merger of their firm, Modus. Appearances by their
superiors are a source of worry, and a man named Ted Shaw,
who is in a sister company, fears the loss of his job; in the end,
ironically, he is promoted to director of the conglomerate firm.

Irony also governs the most sensational plot development,
the death of one of the Modus sales force. Through the play
much has been made of the single-minded devotion to business

of John Garrard, the Modus managing director, a famously driven man: as Frank Prosser says, "Nothing in his head but walls and doors."[20] He is obsessed with detail; he enters the hotel worrying about who sold it its doors; he cuts through the salesmen's evasions about sales to extract their acknowledgment that they have no contracts yet; and he has the absent-mindedness of a person who thinks of nothing but sales. During the course of the next day, he seems to recognize the human attractions of Mrs. Rogers, the long-suffering secretary to his old friend Tom Olley (they have been colleagues for thirty-two years, having met just after the war); after he takes her to dinner, she tells him, "You won't look at yourself. You look at everything but yourself. I can't think what it must be like, being inside that shell. I'd like to help you come out, but you won't, and there's nothing I can do to make you. It's useless to go on talking about it, so I'll go away now, before I start to cry. You wouldn't like that. But I can't bear it, I don't know how to put up with my life" (329–30). They go into the bedroom together and, presumably, make love, though this event is denoted by some surreal action around the display involving the other characters and Garrard's voice, from the bedroom, murmuring: "Eastern Europe. Get into Eastern Europe. Hold Davis off if we get into Eastern Europe. Get that address if we get into Eastern Europe. Get into Eastern Europe if we get into Eastern Europe" (331).

When Garrard, still with Mrs. Rogers, feels chest pains, everyone takes it for granted that he has had the heart attack that his driven, Type-A behavior has long promised; Garrard himself tells Olley, "It's happened, Tom" (336). Ironically nothing much is wrong with Garrard, and Olley is the one who dies, his body being discovered in the display. Frank Prosser sums him up: "Can't believe he won't just suddenly walk through that door, though. One of his big smiles all over his face. All some kind of mistake. Poor bloody Tom. He was a good man. Kind man. Man of great sweetness, great . . . I don't know how we're all going to get by without him." And Garrard harshly responds, "Yes. Could Ian do the job? I suppose you'd be in the running for it, would you?" (358). As the curtain falls, Garrard is obsessively tidying up the display, which still contains his old friend's body.

Garrard's cold obsessiveness chills the others, the stage direction reveals. The play has provided alternatives, in the person of several of the other characters, to his ethos: Anni, the young German woman, who works with them displaying demountable walls during the day and at night is a revolutionary; Hewlett, who is an evangelical Christian; Mrs. Rogers, who is studying Buddhism and tries to communicate the Four Noble Truths to Garrard; and Olley, a gentler, more ethical sort of businessman, who explains why he is a Catholic: "I'll tell you what the use of my religion is, John. It's to keep you out of jail. We've got to have one man on the Board with some kind of morals or we'd have ceased trading years ago" (280).

Karen Blansfield comments that many "critics were troubled by the subplots, weak characterization, or lack of originality" of *Make and Break,* which she calls "one of Frayn's darker plays."[21] Frayn's own analysis of his play is worth quoting at some length:

> I think *Make and Break* is about how we all compulsively exploit the possibilities of the world around us—about how we eat it—how we *have* to eat it—how we transform it into food and clothes and housing, and of course lay it waste in the process. Is Garrard more monstrous than the rest of us?

If he seems so, isn't it because he lacks our saving hypocrisy—because he fails to dissemble the appetites that we all have, that we all *must* have if we are able to survive? I can't help feeling, too, that if the play is seen as some kind of attack upon business, or industrialism, this is merely because it is assumed that no one would ever write about these subjects *without* moral condescension of one sort or another."[22]

Frayn has paid tribute to David Storey's plays, "which demonstrated to me for the first time that the great world of work in which we all live could be represented on the stage."[23] As Karen Blansfield comments, "many of Frayn's own plays concern people at work—including architects, journalists, actors, salesmen, librarians, and bureaucrats—and reveal how professions influence the characters' lives, both in and out of the office."[24] It is difficult to know if *Make and Break* gives an *accurate* impression of what the world of work is like for people who sell products like the Modus line; but it gives an entirely believable one, thick with detail. Whether the detail is the product of research or purely of imagination, one feels in the presence of real door and wall salesmen in the first scene, with the whole staff selling as hard as they can:

> PROSSER: These are *walls*. This is a *wall system*. Fully demountable, fully adjustable walls combined with a range of fully uniform finishes for your load-bearing elements. Movable solid walls. You can't see where the structural element stops and the movable element starts until I unlock it and turn it . . .
>
> . . .
>
> OLLEY: Sound transmission? This core will give you a sound reduction of forty-seven decibels!

. . .

HEWLETT: . . . the standard core is inert European flaxboard, but of course if the overriding consideration is the floor loading, then you're going to choose extruded chipboard as your core option . . .

. . .

OLLEY: . . . mansonia, okoume, paldao, or zebrano, or if you're going to paint it then specify plain birch. The rotary cut is the cheapest, of course, but it you want a clear finish you might find you'd rather go for the quarter cut, which is the straight grain showing the most figuring, or the crown cut, which shows off the heart features of the wood . . .

HEWLETT: I mean, *is* floor loading a consideration? (258–59)

In a way these men are babbling, and it is hard to discern a sense in which what they say is *sincere,* but their expertise is a way of staving off confusion and dissolution, much like Mrs. Rogers's novice Buddhism and Prosser's interest in Beethoven; they combine to create what Leonie Caldicott calls "the atmosphere of blighted quality that gives the play its power to move."[25]

In the introduction to *Plays: 2,* Frayn wrote this common-sense dramatic criticism: "You can classify plays in any number of ways—as comedies or tragedies; as verse or prose, as high comedies, low comedies, black comedies, tragi-comedies; as art or entertainment. But however you do it they all fall into two even more fundamental categories—they are all hits or flops."[26] The "flop" he referred to in that volume was the play variously known as *Balmoral* and *Liberty Hall.* It began as *Balmoral* and was presented in 1978 at the Yvonne Arnaud Theatre in Guildford. Two years later a similar version, called

Liberty Hall, was presented at the Greenwich Theatre; then, rewritten and again called *Balmoral,* it was presented again in 1987, at the Bristol Old Vic. It has also played in Pitlochry (Scotland), Cambridge, Singapore, and other sites. It is notable that none of these is in the West End; while others of Frayn's plays have begun their runs outside the center, the successful ones have then been transferred to a larger venue in London's theater district.

As usual, Frayn is fairly ruthless, perhaps too much so, in diagnosing the play's problem. "I see now, with hindsight, that it couldn't possibly work, because it's based upon an entirely abstract notion, a pure counterfactual—a past that never happened, that never *could* happen."[27] The premise is that Britain, rather than Russia, underwent a Bolshevik revolution in 1917; set in 1937, the play premises that Balmoral, the royal retreat in Scotland, has been turned into a shabby home for British writers and a visitor from Russia (still a bourgeois, capitalist country) has come to see what life is like in the new workers' paradise. The obvious inspiration is the visits made by Europeans such as H. G. Wells and André Gide to the Soviet Union, often so starry-eyed that they saw only what they wanted to see, as well as the author's own visits to the Soviet Union in the 1950s and 1960s. There are several sources of comedy. One is reversal. What if Britain had had the revolution that Russia had? How would people cope? The play explores, chiefly, the relations between workers and bosses, which have changed less than propaganda suggests. There is a Scottish servant who does all the work of Balmoral—very much as in prerevolutionary days.

Another form of reversal comes when this servant, McNab, is forced to impersonate Hugh Walpole, one of the writers in residence, who unfortunately dies during the visit by the Russian

Kochetov and his official guide, Trisha, a great admirer of Walpole's work. Being interviewed by the visitors and having the power that comes from possessing a secret his erstwhile superiors cannot permit him to reveal produces a funny series of shoe-on-the-other-foot moments for McNab and Skinner, the warden of the writers' home, who is forced to impersonate McNab and carry pails of pigswill. Speaking as Walpole, McNab complains bitterly about the treatment of the servant McNab, though he often forgets and says things like "Right. Me it was that was sitting there. Right. So I just sat there, not eating, saying nothing, with a terrible pained expression on his face. On my face. So I said to him, 'What's the trouble, Mr Walpole?' I said to *me,* 'What's the trouble?' *He* said to me, 'What's the trouble?' He, the butler, said to me, Mr Walpole, 'What's the trouble?' "[28]

When the visitors identify McNab as the man they saw carrying pigswill on their arrival, there is a desperate, improvised explanation from two of the resident writers:

> DEEPING: He is very fastidious about his typewriter.
> TRISHA: But you had a bucket of pigswill.
> DEEPING: His typewriter was in a disgusting state.
> BLYTON: He drops bits of food into it as he types. (130)

McNab's self-pity, which he has to disguise as Walpole's concern for the servant McNab, produces an expressive response from Kochetov: "when Mr Walpole speaks about John McNab he becomes eloquent, he becomes passionate. He feels passionate resentment for McNab's wrongs. He feels passionate pride in McNab's ancestry. This—for me—is what the imaginative writer is seeking to do: to enter into the heart and mind of another. And when Walpole talks about McNab he *becomes* McNab! He *is* McNab!" (139).

The play is a farce and, as usual, driven by spiraling panic and the manic stratagems required to avoid exposure. For instance, Walpole's body is hidden in a trunk on the stage, requiring characters to sit on the lid to keep it shut; they jump up, others rush to push the lid back down, and Walpole's leg bursts into view from time to time, fortunately always while the visitors are momentarily looking in another direction.

A final, more subtle source of the play's comedy is the selection of writers inhabiting Balmoral: Hugh Walpole, Godfrey Winn, Dornford Yates, and Enid Blyton. Walpole, who actually died in 1941, was a novelist; Godfrey Winn, a columnist; Dornford Yates (a pseudonym) was a prolific author of, among other things, a series of novels about upper-class adventurers; and Enid Blyton wrote some six hundred books, many of them adventures for children. Her best known works are series—the Famous Five, the Secret Seven—and her first full-length book was published in 1937, the year in which Balmoral is set. In a drunken, sentimental moment of the play, the characters swear to be friends always, and Blyton says, "And it'll be a secret! We'll be the Secret Seven!" (148.) At the end of the play she says to Kochetov, with whom she has fallen in love, " Oh, Volodya! We could be married! I could write children's books! I've always wanted to write for children" (155). Since she is at Balmoral, she must already be an author; in Frayn's counterfactual version, she is a poet, specializing in erotic verse: as McNab sums up her writing, "Smouldering eyes and steaming thighs" (132).

It is hard to see, finally, why *Balmoral* was so pronounced a flop. It is as witty and well constructed as many of Frayn's more well-received farces. His own judgment is that "farce, I now realise, has to be rooted in immediately believable reality. Desperation may eventually drive the characters to the most fantastic and improbable lengths, but the desperation has to be established first, and its source has to be the threat of an embarrassment so familiar that the audiences' palms sweat in sympathy." He concludes, *Balmoral* "was doomed from the first by a fundamental conceptual error. It was a Titanic searching for its iceberg."[29]

In 1982 came what is undoubtedly still Michael Frayn's biggest theatrical success: *Noises Off*. It opened at the Lyric Theatre in Hammersmith in February and moved to the Savoy Theatre in the West End the following month, where it ran for over 1,400 performances, closing only in 1986. It had a long and successful run in the United States, productions in "virtually every country (except Albania and China),"[30] repeated tours throughout Britain, frequent revivals worldwide, and a filmed version in 1992. (The film was an Americanized version of the play, with a star-filled cast including Carol Burnett, Michael Caine, Denholm Elliott, Julie Hagerty, Marilu Henner, Christopher Reeve, John Ritter, and Nicolette Sheridan.) *Noises Off* achieved not only popular success but critical éclat that was, if not universal, then nearly so and in some cases almost ecstatic. To accounts like "an ingeniously synchronized piece of writing and performing . . . [and] a forceful argument for farce's value as human comedy," a "brilliant play, . . . the funniest farce of our day," and "at once an evocation, an interpretation, and a rebirth of that atavistic form, knockabout farce," one could add Brendan Gill's review in the *New Yorker*, which responded to *Noises Off* by declaring that Michael Frayn is

> obviously one of the small handful of geniuses who leap out of the ruck of ordinary writers, such as Dante, Shakespeare, and Goethe, and insist upon making a real mark for themselves in the world. The latest manifestation of Frayn's

astounding talent is a farce so complex in plot and so rapid in execution that Einstein himself would have blanched at the difficulty of following its innumerable anfractuosities.[31]

There were dissenters. Robert Brustein, reviewing the New York production, writes, "Watching this carefully manufactured laugh machine was like spending three hours staring into the works of a very expensive, very complicated Swiss clock—impressive workmanship, but for how long can one look at revolving wheels, moon disks, and star dials?"[32] An academic critic made much of the supposed difficulty of deciding "just exactly what kind of play it is—parody? Travesty? Improvisation?"[33] But Katharine Worth recognized exactly what sort of play it is, declaring, "Frayn emerges in this latest play as a master of the form and *Noises Off* as a farce which proves—if we had doubted it—that the tradition remains unshaken."[34]

Frayn had, of course, written farce before. The two most clever features of *Noises Off* are that it is a farce *about* putting on a farce, and that it shows the behind-the-scenes action involved. A company of third-rate actors is preparing to put on a British sex farce called *Nothing On*. From what the audience sees of *Nothing On* (the play within the play), it will involve many of the staple elements of such long-running plays as *No Sex, Please, We're British* (which has become the eponymous representative of a class of British sex farces that also includes *Run for Your Wife*, *Wife Begins at Forty*, and similar titles): would-be adulterers barely escaping detection by their partners, disguise and mistaken identity, pratfalls, women in their underwear and men whose trousers fall down, and dizzying entrances and exits. There are seven or eight doors in the set, in addition to a window that is also an entrance. There is a supposedly empty house, with two couples sneaking in for sex; one couple owns the house but is supposed to be in Spain for tax reasons, the other consists of a real estate agent (who is pretending to be the owner) and a tax inspector who, unsurprisingly, is handling the first man's case for the Inland Revenue; other participants include the maid and a burglar. All have to try, under conditions of rising panic, to stay out of each other's way and invent explanations to forestall exposure and embarrassment. The company of *Noises Off* also includes three people who are not supposed to appear in *Nothing On* (though eventually they all do): the director, a stage manager, and an assistant stage manager, a dim young woman obviously selected because her father's company is underwriting the production.

The play has three acts. Act 1 consists of the dress rehearsal of *Nothing On,* the day before it is to open in Weston-super-Mare. Nothing goes well. Characters do not know their lines; the nominal star, Dotty Otley, playing the maid, cannot remember what to bring off stage or leave on. (The props, particularly a series of plates of sardines, one of which becomes superglued to an actor, are very important.) Everyone is worried about Selsdon, an elderly actor suspected of being drunk all the time and certainly too deaf and inattentive to follow his cues; simultaneously, the first male lead is torn between two of the actresses, while the second male is known to be having trouble in his marriage. The director, Tim, is himself having affairs with two members of the company and is, moreover, distracted by his need to get back up to London where he will be directing *Richard III.*

The brilliant second act shows the same events (essentially act 1 of *Nothing On* again, though slightly shortened). The players are a month into the tour and are presenting a Wednesday matinee in Goole (a town in South Yorkshire that stands here for the middle of nowhere). But this time the set has been rotated 180 degrees, and the audience is seeing it from backstage. (Frayn may be illustrating the Player's observation, from Tom Stoppard's 1967 *Rosencrantz and Guildenstern Are Dead*: "We do on stage the things that are supposed to happen off. Which is a kind of integrity, if you look on every exit as being an entrance somewhere else."[35]) Just as, when a character on the stage in act 1 enters a room, it is actually an exit from the set, so, in act 2, exits from the set of *Noises Off* (i.e., the backstage of *Nothing On*) are entrances to the set of the play being performed.

David Richards, profiling Frayn for the *Washington Post,* explains the origin of the backstage scene:

> The seeds of "Noises Off" were planted in 1970, when Frayn, then a successful journalist, wrote his first play, a collection of four one-acts for two performers, collectively titled "The Two of Us." One of the plays ["Chinamen"] was a brief farce, in which the two actors played five characters between them.
>
> "The bare minimum of farce is usually three people—two people discovered in a compromising situation by a third," [Frayn] explains, crossing his arms professorially. "So in this case, with only two actors, there were a lot of quick changes and the business of stage managers' arms coming through the door in order to keep the illusion going. One night, I watched it all from behind. And I thought the spectacle of these two actors rushing back and forth from one door to the next, changing costumes as they went, driven by this mad compulsion to get back on stage in time for their entrances, reflected something about the lives we all lead. We all do a certain amount of desperate fixing behind the scenes in order to keep a presentable social front going to the world. We all feel

terrified when it's threatened. And I thought then that I'd like to do something about a farce seen from behind."[36]

The idea that we all are implicated in the manic adjustments and compensations of the backstage of a farce is a striking one. The director of *Nothing On* in *Noises Off* says something similar: "Don't worry. Think of the first night as a dress rehearsal. If we can just get through the play once tonight for doors and sardines. That's what it's all about. Doors and sardines. Getting on—getting off. Getting the sardines on—getting the sardines off. That's farce. That's the theatre. That's life."[37]

The backstage action of act 2 is hectic, complete with the usual sorts of misunderstandings—flowers purchased for one woman accidentally but gratefully received by another, a bottle of whisky moved around to keep it from Selsdon, and understudies going on for missing actors.

Some reviewers found act 3 the weakest part of Frayn's play. In it, the audience once again sees the company play act 1 of *Nothing On,* again from the right side of the scenery. Another two months have passed, it is now Stockton-on-Tees, and everything has become a shambles. The company is tired, and the frictions shown in the first two acts—competition between the actresses for the favors of Garry Lejeune, for instance—pay off in increasingly visible ways. The curtain rises prematurely to reveal the stage manager working on the props. Mrs. Clackett comes on limping from a kick by Belinda and incorporates her grievances into her opening lines (she has answered the telephone):

> Here we are, we haven't been going three months, and already she's lashing out with her feet, and here am I, I don't know where I am, I'm eating sardines off the floor with one knee, don't tell us they've gone again . . .

(*She looks round for the sardines*)

. . . and if you want anything else you'll have to ring the house-agents, because they've got their hands free to see what they're doing. . . . No, they're not in Spain, they're next to the phone in the study. Squire, Squire, Hackham, and hold on, I'm going to do something wrong here, I can't think with one hand. (470–71)

As she leaves, she mistakenly takes the telephone receiver with her, then, as the next actors make their entrance, begins slowly dragging the rest of the phone off stage; eventually it is thrown into the garden and brought back in by later-arriving actors, leaving the cord tangled around part of the set.

As the play continues to disintegrate, lines are omitted, then awkwardly supplied by other actors:

FLAVIA: (*Hurriedly.*) Yes, but Inland Revenue! We must have our little talk first about Inland Revenue! Because you're thinking something like, "If Inland Revenue finds out we're in the country, even for one night, bang goes our claim to be resident abroad. . . . " (478)

When Mrs. Clackett's line is "I thought you was in Spain," her obsession with the sardines produces "I thought you was in Sardinia!" (478). One actor is injured, and on his character's next entrance he is played by Tim, the stage manager; later, Selsdon comes on as the burglar, followed by Tim as the burglar and then Lloyd, the director, also as the burglar, totaling three burglars who speak their lines in unison. This requires Poppy, the assistant stage manager, to play the sheik who has come to view the house. The comic hysteria produces a tumultuous ending. Poppy's entrance provides an irrational way of getting the play ended. She comes on in sheik's robes:

MRS. CLACKETT: Oh, it's the other one! And in her wedding dress!

OMNES: Oh!

FLAVIA: Yes! Yes! It's their wedding day! What a happy ending!

OMNES: Ah!

Lloyd and Poppy are hurriedly ushered down centre.

FLAVIA: They just want to be alone in their new home. If only someone would . . .

She opens the downstairs bathroom door to demonstrate the action to the wings.

. . . pull the blinds!

Enter Tim from the open downstairs bathroom, dressed in the black sheets.

TIM: (*Uncertainly.*) Come on?

MRS. CLACKETT: Oh, and here's the mother of the bride!

TIM: Go off?

OMNES: (*Demonstrating.*) Pull the blinds!

Exit Tim into the wings.

BURGLAR SELSDON: Last line?

OMNES: Last line!

BURGLAR SELSDON: (*Crosses to Vicki.*) But I'll tell you one thing, Vicki.

Slaps her on the back, and she loses her lenses.

OMNES: What's that, Dad?

BURGLAR SELSDON: When all around is strife and uncertainty, there's nothing like . . .

Takes the sardines.

. . . a good old-fashioned plate of curtain!

> *Down comes the curtain—and jams just above the level*
> *of their heads. As one man they seize hold of it and drag*
> *it down to the ground.* (494)

It can be argued that act 3 adds nothing crucial to what has been revealed in acts 1 and 2. And yet it is wildly funny. One of the principles of farce is incremental repetition. In the play-within-a-play, if done properly, this should include the multiplication of plates of sardines. In *Noises Off,* it includes the brilliant multiplication of burglars and the multiplication of ways this troupe of actors can become hopelessly entangled in *Nothing On.*

Reviewers have repeatedly commented on Frayn's consummate exploitation of the features of farce, giving him credit for reviving an outdated form. Having written in *Noises Off* something like the farce to end all farces, summing up the genre, making fun of it while using it for ingenious comic effect, he may have felt the need to move in a different direction with his next play. Whatever the reason, *Benefactors: A Play in Two Acts* (1984) is a significant departure from the kind of plays of which *Noises Off* is a sort of culmination. As Karen Blansfield sums it up, "The somber sophistication of this play startled many theatre-goers after the hilarious antics of *Noises Off,* and [Frank] Rich [reviewer for the *New York Times*] found it 'hard to fathom' that the two plays 'were written by the same man.' . . . Darker and more complex than Frayn's earlier works, *Benefactors* is also more topical . . . and its intricate structure prompted comparisons to Henrik Ibsen's *The Master Builder* and to Anton Chekhov."[38] The comparison to Chekhov might have stemmed from Frayn's translation/adaptation of *Wild Honey* opening three months after *Benefactors,* becoming the third Frayn play to be running at the same time in the West End.

In addition to a noticeably darker tone than most of the plays that had preceded it, *Benefactors* has a looser form than Frayn had previously used, with a small cast (four characters), a starker set and fewer props (in both of these ways it harkens back to *Clouds*), and more direct addresses by the actors to the audience. Frayn's plays up to this point had operated on the fourth-wall convention, that is, the pretense that the three-walled playing space is actually an enclosed, realistic room, separated from the audience by a wall that, though imaginary, is treated as real; even in *Clouds,* where the characters have what amounts to a series of soliloquies that are spoken aloud in isolation, the "justification" for their soliloquizing is that they are supposed to be reading out what they have written. They are not overtly speaking to the audience. In *Benefactors,* by contrast, there are scenes like this one, with David and Colin recapitulating past action; both are on stage, but speaking to the audience (self-justification in the eyes of the audience seems part of the reason for this device). The entrance of Jane restores interaction between the characters, which is taking place at the point in time (in the past) of which David and Colin are speaking:

> COLIN: I sometimes thought about David, hunched over his drawing-board far into the night, and I couldn't help laughing. He was using up his life designing a scheme that was never going to be built. That everyone but him knew was never going to be built. That he knew was never going to be built.
>
> DAVID: I could have done with some help from Jane. No, that was unfair. No reason why she should have to work for me if she didn't want to. Better for her to have her own job. And if she was going to start preserving

things, better for her to be preserving them over in Wandsworth.

Exit DAVID left.

COLIN: I did one fair and tidy thing, though. I suggested the name of an excellent field-worker to our friends in Wandsworth. I gave Jane her start in life, at any rate.

Exit COLIN right.

Enter JANE centre.

JANE: David not back?

Enter SHEILA left.

SHEILA: He's over the road.[39]

Benefactors is a study of marriage and of idealism. The main benefactor, perhaps, is David, or at least he is the one who is most uncomplicatedly dedicated to benefaction, until the end. He is an architect who has been given the assignment of designing new housing for a decayed neighborhood of south London, Basuto Road. He is consistently torn between two imperatives: he wants to design and build attractive and pleasant housing for a population that needs it; but he must put homes for hundreds of families on a limited space. Initially he is determined not to build tower blocks: "I'm not going to go high. But if I don't go high we won't qualify for the high-rise subsidy. . . . But when I think of all the struggle it's going to be! When I think of all the words, all the paper, all the anger, all the dust, all the mud. . . . Because I'm not going to build towers. No one wants to live in a tower" (8–9). David knows what the people want: they want, as Colin puts it, "nice little semis with nice little gardens" (6). But nice little semidetached houses don't utilize space well.

The play demonstrates David's gradual and heartbreaking surrender to conditions. He must go high; and, gradually, because of the slow discovery of the awkward placement of electric lines, and planning regulations, legal restrictions, and other forms of entropy, he must go higher and higher.

From the beginning, his plans are ridiculed by Colin, married to Sheila. An old college friend and his current neighbor, Colin writes for a women's magazine and has a malicious attitude toward David's work. This is complicated by the strain of his marriage to the needy and somewhat helpless Sheila, who not only depends on Jane (David's wife, her benefactor) to get food on the table and collect her children from school, but is a little in love with David and eventually becomes his assistant. This is part of David's role as benefactor: he longs to help the people of Basuto Road, he longs to help Sheila, he longs to help Colin long even after he knows that Colin is his enemy.

The precipitating incident comes when David talks expansively to Sheila about the plan he has now been reduced to. No more thought of not going high:

Skyscrapers, Sheila. That's the solution. That's the only answer. I've tried every other solution, and it doesn't work. I'm going to build 150 low-rise walk-ups for families with young children, and then 600 units for all the rest in twin skyscrapers. What do you think? I don't mean eleven stories, or eighteen, or twenty-four. I mean fifty stories. The highest residential buildings in Europe. . . . I feel dizzy just thinking about them. When the clouds are low they'll be above the clouds. . . . They'll be a hazard to aircraft. Sheila! So what do you think! They'll change the whole climate! I'm joking, Sheila. (38–39)

Colin, with whom Sheila shares this vision (without the irony), passes it on to the newspapers and precipitates a vigorous protest against the building project; when Sheila leaves him, he goes to the area proposed for redevelopment, lives as a squatter, and leads the protest, which is ultimately successful.

The most complicated character in *Benefactors* is Jane. Impatient with both Colin and Sheila, for different reasons, she loves her husband but increasingly agrees with Colin about Basuto Road. She goes to work with a trust that renovates housing—a sort of implicit criticism of her husband's willingness to clear it all away for utopian construction, which he construes as a betrayal. The vote to kill David's plan leads to a muted ending to the play in which David is first emotionally crushed but then goes to work designing rehabilitation schemes for Jane's trust, including those in Basuto Road, one early result of which is Colin's eviction. So what is learned? David becomes disillusioned about people, claiming that it wasn't Colin, or the electricity board, or the Council's cowardice that doomed his plans: "It was people. That's what wrecks all our plans—people." Jane admits that "I suppose that's when we ceased to believe in change" (69).

There is some improvement; Sheila is being rehabilitated by psychiatry as the play ends, and David expresses some modest satisfaction and pride in the work he is doing, though nothing like the excitement evident in act 1. There has been a good deal of critical discussion about the theme of *Benefactors,* with a tendency to see it as a criticism of the idealism (or maybe the arrogant condescension) of the 1960s (the Basuto Road plans, and their destruction, take place in 1968 and 1969). Frayn has addressed this question in two interesting statements to interviewers: when John L. DiGaetani suggested that *Benefactors* was "an attack on the well-meaning but arrogant liberal of the sixties," Frayn disagreed strenuously:

> No, no. Not in any way at all. I never write attacks. It's just about the difficulties of trying to help people, and the play also tried to show the difficulties of being helped. Helping people is not an easy task, and the people in *Benefactors* don't carry it off very well. The play was also about a change which has occurred in Europe, and I think in America as well, since the sixties, and a shift from the feeling that we could actually change society, which I believe was the commonly accepted wisdom at the time by most people. I think that view has largely disappeared and we are more pessimistic now.[40]

He made the same point about loss of faith in the possibility of rational human solutions to social problems in 2003 and added, "We began to see that some problems are endemic in the human condition, that conflict is endemic in human societies, that you can't have human society without conflict. That is what *The Benefactors* is about."[41] Significantly, he is not talking just about solving the problems of bad housing, or helping people to live more rewarding lives; the inevitability of conflict and the difficulty of helping people, or indeed being helped, link the inhabitants of Basuto Road with Colin and Sheila, David and Jane, the problems of marriage with those of public housing. The personal may not be the political, but in *Benefactors* it suffers from the same inexorable limitations presented by human nature.

Michael Frayn's translation/adaptation of Chekhov's play, performed as *Wild Honey,* the title given to it by Frayn, was a great success in London, though not in New York, and Frayn comments on its opening night: "I suppose, looking back, that the glorious first night in London marked the climax of my career in the theatre." (This was written in 1991, and he has had enormous successes unanticipated then.) "*Benefactors* had opened three months earlier at the Vaudeville, *Noises Off* was still running across the road at the Savoy; for just over a year, until August 1985, when *Wild Honey* closed, I had three plays on in London. Since then I have done almost nothing in the theatre but straight translations, and one new play, *Look Look*."[42] His new, original work for the remainder of the 1980s consisted of a theatrical film, *Clockwise;* a new production of *Balmoral*, which was a substantial revision of the play performed as *Liberty Hall* in 1980, which was itself very close to the play put on as *Balmoral* in 1978; and a television play, *First and Last*.

Clockwise was released in 1986. The director was Christopher Morahan; the producer, Michael Codron, has also produced many of Frayn's stage plays. *Clockwise* starred John Cleese, whose gift for physical comedy was well displayed in the film. Because it was not limited to a stage set there were more opportunities for comic mischance, including car accidents, mistakes at the train station, getting lost in fields.

The premise of *Clockwise* is that Brian Stimpson, the headmaster of a mixed comprehensive school (i.e., a state-maintained, rather than selective, fee-paying secondary school) has been elected chairman of the headmasters' conference. The day of the play is his big day; he is to travel to Norwich, where the headmasters are meeting at the University of East Anglia, to accept his election to this office, and from the time he awakens he is practicing his speech. Stimpson is a punctilious, detail-obsessed martinet; he believes that exact attention to time and scheduling is the key to his success. The film establishes early that he frequently says "Right," in a tone of great decisiveness, and this is the key to his problems, since he becomes confused at the station over whether his train is on the right or left platform. He goes wrong, and he misses the train. A long, intricate, and increasingly bizarre series of accidents follows. His wife, Gwenda, has driven to her volunteer work with elderly people, so he cannot take the car. Stimpson finds one of his pupils, a sixteen-year-old girl, skipping school and persuades her to drive him to Norwich, though not telling her the truth about where they are going. The car is wrecked, the police are involved; he is suspected of kidnapping the girl (by her parents) and running away with her for an illicit entanglement (by Gwenda, whose offer to accompany him to Norwich Stimpson had refused). Along the way he meets a woman whom he knew when he was in school, and he drags her away as well. (She reveals that as a youth he was chaotic and unpunctual, shedding some light perhaps on how he became so insistently the reverse as an adult.) Parts of the car belonging to the family of the teenaged Laura, who is not a licensed driver, come off; they get stuck in a field and have to be pulled out by a tractor. In a monastery, Stimpson takes a bath and dons monastic robes, then a stolen suit, which, when he gives his speech, has the sleeves attached with tape that, naturally, fails. His rising hysteria is of course driven by worry about the time.

The momentum of the film and the suspiciousness of Stimpson's activities (which are perfectly logical to him) bring almost all of the characters of the play, including Gwenda, several of her dotty old ladies, Mr. Jolly, who teaches at Stimpson's school, and the police, to the headmasters' conference. The speech itself was left on the wrong train, but his attempts to deliver it are drowned out anyway.

Clockwise is an excellent demonstration of Frayn's explanation of the emotional content of farce:

I think what most farces have in common is the element of panic. People lose their heads. They find themselves in an embarrassing situation, and they tell a lie to cover up. The lie doesn't make things better, it makes them worse, and they then have to explain not only the initial embarrassing situation but the lie as well, and the panic escalates.[43]

First and Last is a different sort of play altogether. A television play about a retired man who walks from Land's End to John O'Groats (that is, from the southwestern-most to northeastern-most points in Great Britain), it was based on the accomplishment of the author's cousin, and Frayn writes in an author's note, "All the characters and events in this film are fictitious. But it was my cousin's feat that set this fiction off in the first place, and I should like to think that a little of his tenacity and modesty, and of the courage with which he faced illness, are reflected in it."[44] *First and Last* was televised on BBC1 on December 12, 1989.

Alan Holly, the main character, is a retiree who has spent years talking about his plans for walking the length of Britain when he retired, without any very strong desire to really do it; now that he is retired, he is making the trip out of a feeling of obligation. He is not much of a walker and is in ill health anyway (perhaps an ulcer, more likely cancer in his abdomen). He leaves behind his wife, Audrey, and two children, Stephen and Sandra. Stephen's wife, Lisa, and their three children and their sitter, Shana, and Sandra and her husband (called Sandra's Stephen) and *their* two children are the choral characters in the play, which works by alternating scenes of Alan's progress and scenes of his family, who track his progress on maps, worry about him, and become exasperated by his stubbornness. The dual focus reveals interesting family changes, including, for instance, a growing friendship between Lisa and Sandra. Alan's walk is difficult; at one point he gives up and comes home, but after spending the night there thinks better of it, returns to the exact point where he had quit and resumes his trek. He weakens in Yorkshire and spends time with a farm family; just as Audrey arrives to rescue him, he sets off again. In Scotland he has to go to the hospital. Eventually, though, he makes it to John O'Groats.

There is comedy in *First and Last,* some of it stemming from the frustration of Alan's family, some of it from the couple across the road, Laurence and Ivy (Laurence is dismissive of Alan's abilities but when he, who seldom moves from the house, tries to go a short distance down the road to buy sprouts, he ends up in the emergency room), some from Alan's efforts to make his adventures sound more interesting than they are. For instance,

> (ALAN, *walking, followed by an unexplained small dog. He passes various abandoned factories and a decaying Wesleyan chapel.*)

ALAN: (*Voice-over.*) Good. No, quite something, the Black Country. I've always rather wanted to, you know. . . .

AUDREY: (*Voice-over.*) Yes, well as long as it's nice country. They all send their love, of course.

ALAN: (*Voice-over, into phone, ironically.*) Some of the architecture round here is rather interesting.

> *He passes a shop called "Fags and Mags."*

Rather quaint names you see written up.

. . .

AUDREY: You are, you know—eating properly? Lots of . . . ?

ALAN: Yes, yes.

AUDREY: Not all just . . . ?

ALAN: No, no.

He goes into a fish and chip shop called "The Frying Scotsman." (44–45)

But the comedy is low key, and the predominant note is sadness, because of the growing feeling that Alan's accomplishment, while brave and impressive, not only is misunderstood by his family and friends, but may be his last act of defiance of fate. In the Scottish hospital, the doctor clearly thinks something worse than an ulcer is causing his pain.

ALAN: (*Doggedly.*) The ulcer?

CASUALTY OFFICER: (*Smiles.*) We'll see.

Nods at the backpack.

Walking holiday?

ALAN *nods. The casualty officer puts the letter [to his physician, recommending a referral to a specialist] in his hands.* ALAN *looks at it sombrely, then up at the* CASUALTY OFFICER.

CASUALTY OFFICER: (*Smiles.*) No more walking, Mr Holly.

Go home. Plenty of rest. Get your strength up. (82)

And the play ends both anticlimactically (all the family but Audrey gather for a welcome-home party that Alan misses by having been delayed a day) and ambiguously. He sees Audrey waiting for him at John O'Groats. They meet wordlessly; she notices him wincing in pain.

Then they walk very slowly, hand in hand, past a souvenir kiosk with a sign pointing to it saying, "First and Last House in Scotland." He looks at the sign, then stops and gives his

camera to AUDREY. *He goes over to stand next to the words,*
"First and Last" on the kiosk itself. AUDREY *puts the camera*
to her eye, then takes it away again to demonstrate a smile.
ALAN *attempts a smile. By the time the shutter clicks the smile*
has begun to fade. The image becomes motionless, the life
and definition drain away. All that remains is the snapshot of
a gaunt, aging man with the trace of a smile around his lips.
(96)

Frayn's next play contains his most determined assault on the
fourth-wall convention, with a fluid interchange between audience and actors. Perhaps that assault was too determined. *Look
Look,* produced in 1990, contains a playwright character called
Keith, who sits in the auditorium watching a performance of his
own play. This permits wry commentary on the obstructions
and misunderstandings of the audience around him. Early in act
1 he observes, "Oh, and an empty seat. Only been running for
four months, and already there's an empty seat in Row G.
. . . My God, there's two more in Row F."[45] Keith's distress is
ironic. *Look Look,* unlike the play-within-a-play, survived for
only twenty-seven performances, though it was scheduled for a
run of a year at the Aldwych Theatre in the West End. It failed
in several different ways. Others of Frayn's plays had opened
inauspiciously: *The Two of Us* had certainly received some bad
reviews and negative reaction from theater-goers when it
opened in 1970, but it was a box-office success and ran for six
months despite its being by a playwright with no established
name in the theater. Frayn's second play, *The Sandboy,* had
closed after twenty-five performances in 1971 and has been
withdrawn from performance and publication; again, this was
an early work of which less was expected. *Look Look,* on the
other hand, was Frayn's first original work for the stage since

the enormous success of *Noises Off* and the less sensational but still very solid success of *Benefactors*. In 1996 Karen Blansfield explained that *Look Look* "was a major flop that no doubt contributed to Frayn's subsequent withdrawal from the stage,"[46] an account that probably seemed accurate at the time not only to her but to the author himself (though "withdrawal" may make it sound too voluntary). In the introduction to *Plays: 2*, Frayn calls it "too humiliatingly unsuccessful even to reproduce here in the flops department" and speculated that a playwright's success usually lasted no more than fifteen years: "My first play, *The Two of Us*, was produced in 1970, so maybe my grand climax was also my final curtain."[47] And in his introduction to *Plays: 3*, he again referred to his failure, writing that "the failure of *Look Look* in 1990 had put an abrupt end to the successes of the eighties."[48]

For not only was *Look Look* a poor draw to audiences, it was badly received by critics. And, as Frayn comments, "It is very galling to get bad reviews for a play and feel they're completely unjustified. It's even more galling to get bad reviews and feel that the critics are absolutely right."[49] The major objection was to the complexity and consequent obscurity of the play. Irvine Wardle writes that "Frayn's energy goes into tortuous ingenuity; the spectator's energy goes into trying to unscramble it. There is not much left over for laughter." Other reviewers complained that it was "when Mr. Frayn attempted to push his ambition beyond the bounds of our credulity and to the outer edges of theatre convention that everything begins to come unstuck" and wondered how the author "thought such an amorphous mass would be a rewarding study for a play."[50] *Look Look* confused the audience; and it is confusing to read as well.

It seems at first an inverse *Noises Off.* Where that play broke the frame in order to reveal the reality behind the artifice, showing in act 1 how the play was put together and in act 2 what happened backstage while it was being performed, in *Look Look* the audience looks "through" the stage in the other direction, at the audience. As the curtain rises the "real" audience finds itself looking through a proscenium at the seats in a theater, which gradually fill with the players. This is act 1, which takes the audience up to the interval, or intermission, of the play they are watching. (The nature of this play can only be inferred from the audience's reaction—dismay at scenes of violence or sex, Keith's expectations of laughs and tears.) Act 2 complicates matters very greatly, and it is that which introduces the confusing ingenuity into the play; several minutes into it, with the "audience" back in their seats (but in fact replaced by doubles), the set changes, so that instead of looking through a fourth wall at the "audience," the real audience in the theater is now looking both at a stage and across it to the seats beyond. Thus there are two arenas for the action: the auditorium, as in act 1, and the stage on which the play is going on. The interaction between these two worlds is the subject of the remainder of the play.

The repetition in the title *Look Look* suggests, whether intentionally or not, this division, but it is hard to detect an integral relationship between the two acts. Act 1 is made up of funny observations about the behavior of theatrical audiences *as* audiences—one elderly American sleeps through the play, another old woman talks to her daughter about home furnishings, people cough, go in and out, rustle candy wrappers, complain that an understudy is performing instead of the star, get into the wrong seats, and so on.[51] A long career of theatergoing will supply such observations, and Frayn has connected them wittily, accompanied by irritated comments from Keith, the playwright whose play the audience—which has presumably come to watch it—is instead obstructing. Besides their various small misbehaviors as audience members, the characters are involved in other human interplay. A man and woman are having an adulterous affair. Another woman, there with her mother, knows the adulterer through her husband. A drama teacher has brought a teenaged boy whom he clearly plans to seduce; instead, the boy clicks with a teenaged girl, sitting with her insufferable parents, and the teenagers run off together during the interval. It is unfair, perhaps, to dismiss all this, as one reviewer did, as "a couple of sketches pasted together by some neat lines and nice acting";[52] but act 1 is funny without being particularly incisive about anything.

It is in act 2 that the confusion of the real and the theatrical begins—a theme that induced several reviewers to invoke Luigi Pirandello. The stage directions indicate this doubling; first, part of the set slides to establish a stage, set for a garden party, between the "auditorium" part of the set and the real audience:

> *Three bells, and the cast of* KEITH's *play, who look precisely like the cast of our play, begin his second act. It bears a striking resemblance to the beginning of the second act of our own play that we have just been watching, a remarkable tribute to the accuracy with which his play reflects the lives of its audience. In fact it is precisely the same, except that the text has been somewhat shortened and the playing is somewhat more theatrical. We are also watching it from behind, because it is being played upstage, towards the upstage audience. (46)*

The script as published has two columns of text to encompass the two actions going on simultaneously. There are some ironic juxtapositions and exchanges between these two "plays," some comic, *Noises Off*–like bits like the substitution of a fake plaster ice-cream cone for a real one, and some explanation, though intermittent, for what has happened, as when Helena, a distracted woman in her forties, becomes uneasy and wonders:

> HELENA: But what's happened to us? Why are we all being so . . . I don't know . . . so stupid? Why don't we know where we are? Why aren't we behaving like normal human beings? Why are we waving our arms about? Why are we saying things? People don't go round saying things!
>
> KEITH: I don't know what you're all complaining about.
>
> *They all turn to look at him.*
>
> You're the lucky ones. Out of the entire audience . . .
>
> *He indicates us.*
>
> . . . you're the ones I've chosen to be upgraded. (58–59)

The play ends with awards given to audience members for such achievements as being best latecomers or Sleeper of the Year, and a reciprocal one for Keith, the author,

> From all those who only sit and look, to the man who first looked out in the darkness and noticed us looking back. A modest theatrical symbol of the dissolving of the darkness and the breaking down of artificial barriers. A simple . . .
>
> *He takes the knitting from Eileen and presents it to Quentin [apparently a mistake for Keith].*
>
> . . . melted choc-ice!
>
> *They all applaud.* (110)

Look Look is challenging, and not just because of the parallel actions, the doubling of characters, and the mirror-image of the audience; it also lacks coherence, and, though the observations about the foibles of theatergoers are comical in their way, the metaphysical point about the relationship between reality and artifice is unclear. There have been plays before in which the audience confronted the auditorium beyond the stage (for instance, Tom Stoppard's *The Real Inspector Hound*), and Pirandello's *Six Characters in Search of an Author* is the classic work built on distinction between "characters" and "persons" and the question of which are more real. *Look Look* is less successful than these in making a dramatic whole of its metatheatrical plot.

CHAPTER 6

Plays since 1990

Most of the 1990s fell into what Frayn calls "the rather bleak part of my career that followed after the failure of *Look Look* in 1990 had put an abrupt end to the successes of the eighties," a time during which he did seem to have "withdrawn" from the theater.[1] His 1993 play, *Here,* was also unsuccessful. Although he published good and well-received novels in 1991 (*A Landing on the Sun*) and 1992 (*Now You Know*), there was little original work for the theater. He adapted (or adapted back) his novel *Now You Know* into a play staged in 1995; he published *Plays: 2* (1991) with a rueful introduction, written in the apparent belief that he was summing up a theatrical career at or near its end. As the century came to a close, however, the arc of his career was changed with the enormous success of his play *Copenhagen,* which appeared at almost the same time as his novel *Headlong,* also a great critical success. Once again he was at the top of his profession in two different genres.

But *Here,* produced in 1993, was not much of a recovery after *Look Look.* It was put on at the Donmar Warehouse and ran for about six weeks. As if in reaction against the fiendishly complicated staging and playing of its predecessor, *Here* is a starker work. It offers one set, a cast of three, a modest amount of scenery. Though it may be wrong to call its technique minimalist (especially by contrast with the earlier *Clouds* or the later *Copenhagen* or *Democracy*), the drama has been reduced to two characters, sometimes joined by a third, on the stage talking.

In act 1, Cath and Phil inspect a flat and, after great difficulty, decide to take it; in act 2, they move out of it. In between they talk to their landlady and downstairs neighbor, Pat, whose husband had used the room.

Much of the dialogue is of this sort:

PHIL: Hold on.
CATH: What?
PHIL: What's going on?
CATH: What do you mean, what's going on?
PHIL: Why are you being like this all of a sudden?
CATH: Like what?
PHIL: Like this.
CATH: Come on.

She opens the door.

PHIL: Just a moment.

He closes the door.

CATH: Do you mind?

She opens the door.

PHIL: I do mind.

He closes the door.

CATH: I want to go.

She opens the door.

PHIL: I don't want to go.

He closes the door.

Not until you tell me.
CATH: Tell you what?
PHIL: What this is all about.[2]

The circular and unprogressive—and remarkably flat—dialogue and the indecisiveness have a slight suggestion of Samuel Beckett. One reviewer invoked both Beckett and Harold Pinter in a negative review that began, "We all took our rubber truncheons to Michael Frayn's last play, *Look Look,* attacking it for its clotted structure and excessive artifice. Clearly in retaliatory mood, he reduces drama in his new play to its simplest ingredients: a young couple existentially defining themselves and their relationship through their occupation of a room."[3] (He went on to judge the play "inherently undramatic.") But citations of Beckett are misleading. Not only do Phil and Cath actually do things (though with some difficulty)—they move into the flat, they move out, though projects like disposing of a chair or telling Pat to stop calling so often remain undone—and not only is the bare stage of act 1 bare because it is an empty apartment that will be furnished in act 2; but there are philosophical concerns at work in *Here* that are not absurdist. In his introduction to the play, Frayn wrote:

> People had leapt to the conclusion [on the basis of the first scene, he believes, from which the above quotation comes] that it was to be an evening about the impossibility of human communication, the failure of feeling, and the meaninglessness of life; whereas it seemed to me about he way we do actually construct a world and a life for ourselves.[4]

Comparisons to Pinter are also beside the point. Cath and Phil are acutely aware of the subtext of their remarks and scrutinize them carefully (often with what seems to be excessive eagerness for hurt feelings), but as far as one can tell they actually love each other and are not engaged in some obscure and indirect struggle for mastery. It is true that they squabble over territory, including where the mattress ought to be in the room and which area, adjacent to the mattress, counts as each individual's "bit" of the room.

But what the play seems most centrally to be about is language and decision-making. Phil has special words, like "authentic" and "over-determinate," which he uses in an attempt to gain advantage in argument (though they are not shown to achieve this aim); he calls for their dialogue to proceed "logically." Ironically, though, Cath and Phil speak as vaguely, some of the time, as any characters in drama. Phil tells Cath, "You're being all like that again" (87). They use the word "thing" freely, as in Phil's question, "What do you mean, it was exactly the same with the other thing? What other thing?" (69). Similarly,

> PHIL: *I've* got a thing tomorrow. That doesn't stop me doing things today. . . . On it goes. On and on. Taking it as it comes. A moment at a time. Living every minute to the full.
> CATH: *You've* got a thing tomorrow? You haven't got a thing tomorrow.
> PHIL: I've got a thing tomorrow.
> CATH: I don't know what you're talking about. (86)

And again,

> CATH: Where were you?
> PHIL: Nowhere. Here. Soup?
> CATH: Soup. Yes.
> PHIL: What?
> CATH: Nothing
> PHIL: In the thing?
> CATH: In the thing.

> *He picks up the toy dog, tosses it behind the curtain,*
> *then crosses to the kitchenette and starts to heat the soup.*
> (99–100)

The dialogue between Cath and Phil demonstrates two seemingly opposed traits. One is that people who know each other can communicate with language whose vagueness will make it opaque to others, or to an audience. But yet they frequently cross-examine each other, seeking the underlying meaning of words and claims, and apparently pretending to be more baffled than they really are. This, too, is realistic.

And they venture into some curiously metaphysical speculations. One is about the nature of the present, as Cath, speaking to Phil, says "It's still *now*. . . . Now. . . . Now. . . . More now . . ." (99). Both are concerned with whether reality is independent of the observer; Phil launches an experiment to see if the clock's hands move only when they are looking at it, and Cath says, when Phil is behind a curtain, "I don't know, do I, if I can't see you. . . . Can't touch you, can't hear you. . . . I don't even know if you exist. . . . Not logically. Do I . . . ? Perhaps you don't exist. Perhaps you never did exist . . . Phil . . . ? Love . . . ?" (99) Phil employs what linguistic philosophers call the use-mention distinction, when he says

> PHIL: So what do you want me to say? "I love you"?
> CATH: No, I've given up on that.
> PHIL: I've just said it. (64)

The problem that occupies most of their analytical attention is what it means to decide.

> PHIL: *You've* thought about us. *I've* thought about us.
> *We've* thought about us. We're us. That's fixed. That's

the problem. It's how we think about everything else. How *we* think about everything else. How we think as *us*. How we shape our world. How we decide.

CATH: How we decide?

PHIL: That's what this is all about. Isn't it?

CATH: You mean how *you* decide.

PHIL: No. How *we* decide. How you and I decide.

CATH: Oh. Well, don't worry about me. I've decided.

PHIL: You've *decided? You've* decided? Cath!

CATH: One of us has to decide. One of us has to decide *something!* And if *you're* not going to decide then *I'm* going to decide, and I've decided.

PHIL: Decided what?

CATH: Decided no. So, off we go.

PHIL: Hold on. (14)

This decision-making, which is about taking the flat, goes on much, much longer, through reversals in which Phil decides no and Cath yes and a stage in which they agree but he dismisses her agreement as inauthentic. Later versions of the same activity involve going out or staying in, where to keep a toy dog, and the placement of the mattress; the one with apparently the most consequence, about having children, leads into the beginning of an infinite regress:

CATH: So what are we deciding about children?

PHIL: We're not deciding.

CATH: Aren't we?

PHIL: Not now.

CATH: So when are we going to decide?

PHIL: I don't know. We'll have to decide.

CATH: Decide when to decide?

PHIL: Of course.

CATH: So when are we going to . . . ?

PHIL: Decide when to decide? We'll have to decide. (58)

Perhaps on the stage this sort of dialogue seems like logic chopping, and reviewers were hard on it as "a numbing form of repeat-speak with pedantic, humourless work-play" or a "steady drip of monosyllabic questions and fudged answers."[5] But there is something central to human relationship in it. Lindsay Duguid, in one of the good notices *Here* received, writes about the "high-risk bits of staging," which include Phil's protracted nose-picking, that "these moments derive a good bit of their impact from their immediacy—which is what makes *Here* a proper piece of theatre rather than just an exceptionally well-written sitcom. That and the recurring swells of sadness which the play orchestrates over the passing of our lives."[6]

Frayn's next stage play was *Now You Know,* which opened in July 1995. This was, of course, a theatrical version of his 1992 novel of the same name. Frayn has frequently commented on the somewhat mysterious way in which a story he imagined turns out to be a novel or a play. It is unusual, then, for one of his works to be both. In light of the concerns of *Here,* it is interesting to see how he decides:

> Since I have spent my life writing novels as well as plays, one of the questions which people always ask is how I decide whether a new idea is one for a play or for a novel. The answer is that I don't. The matter decides itself. The idea that takes shape inside one's head has its form written upon it; that's what makes it an idea and not just a piece of wishful thinking. The one exception to this simple rule is *Now You Know,* which in its time has been both a novel and a play.[7]

He goes on to explain that he originally wrote it as a play but turned it into a novel when he concluded that it was necessary for the audience to know the characters' private thoughts. The novel's technique, in fact, brings together many first-person accounts of events, with all of the different shadings, dramatic irony, mixed motives, and deceptions of self and others, revealed to the reader through the comparison of several partial accounts that multiple inside views afford. Later, Frayn reconsidered and realized that the play could, after all, work as a play, that is, with only the actions and speeches of the characters: "where one sees only as much of each person as he or she chooses to reveal—or fails to keep concealed. Which is of course how we are forced to see the people around us, all the time we are not writing novels about them."[8] That last reflection, while true, does not lead to a decision to make all his later novels plays instead, so the motive for making it a play—the idea that plays are closer to real human experience, limited to what can be seen and heard, with other peoples' minds always inaccessible—explains only so much. Is it possible that the plot of *Now You Know,* which is after all about openness and secrecy, contributed to the decision to rewrite it in a different genre?

In other words, how much openness is enough? Terry's vision of Heaven (used at least in part to seduce Hilary) survives in a reduced form:

> You know what is says about heaven in the Bible—it's built of gold. You know that—everyone knows that. But what sort of gold? You don't know, Hilary, do you. I'll tell you: gold like unto clear glass. . . . Transparent gold. All the walls of all the houses in heaven. A golden light in all the rooms. Nothing hidden. Everything visible.[9]

And of course Terry and even Hilary, who interprets his call for openness more single-mindedly than he does, acknowledge the limits on transparency and exposure.

Making this story into a play removes some of its complexity. Without the inner life given her by the novel, Jacqui is more of a comic stereotype, a wealthy suburban woman with her silly talk of Poops and Pippy and Bicky and Scrumps (some them her daughters, others her ponies); likewise, Kevin and Keith in the mailroom (which is soundproofed so that they are an unheard commotion much of the time) and Shireen on the telephone (she also has a soundproofing device, so when she slides her glass door she is invisible and inaudible) are reduced to lesser and mostly comic roles. Terry's ex-wife has vanished, and other elements are lost to simplification and dramatization as well. Roy, who introduces Hilary and Terry, is of negligible consequence. The action is intensified, taking place entirely within the OPEN offices and focusing ever more strongly on two issues: one of them, Hilary's decision to leave the Home Office, bringing the secret files on the Hassam case with her, and Terry's tergiversation about whether to make them public; the other, the affair between Terry and Hilary, Jacqui's ignorance and then awareness of it, along with Liz's complicity, and its consequences for the movement. All of the important symbolic echoes of *opened* and *closed* remain: the jimmying open of Jacqui's desk, the rifling of Kevin's backpack, revealing his pornography stash, and the secrecy of OPEN's accounts, which, when opened, reveal that without Jacqui's backing the operation will close.

In a perceptive review, Nicholas Lezard wrote:

> *Now You Know,* the play, is sleek and deceptive, like the cliché; the knowledge passed on when you wrap facts up by saying "now you know" is often either inferred or

unwelcome, and carries with it the suggestion that whatever it is should probably have been hidden in the first place. It is the perfect title for the play, and it was the perfect title for Frayn's novel of the same name.[10]

Later in 1995, Frayn's translation/adaptation of Jacques Offenbach's *La Belle Vivette* was performed by the English National Opera. His next original work for the stage was *Copenhagen*, which opened in 1998 and was a sensational success. It revived a career about which he had felt resigned after *Look Look*, and it launched a new kind of Michael Frayn play that (though he has not abandoned the older kind) was to be on view again in *Democracy* (2003). Both of these works deal with real people and the events of modern European history. They are not simply transcriptions of it, and because *Copenhagen* is set during the World War II and is partly about the Third Reich, Frayn's work has become embroiled in contentious arguments about its fidelity to fact. Finally, perhaps because of their subject matter, *Copenhagen* and *Democracy* are not comedies. There is humor in each, characters deliver witty lines, situations reveal their own ironies, but they are worlds away from a play like *Noises Off,* called by Robert Brustein a "laugh-machine." *Copenhagen* is Frayn's most significant play since *Noises Off*. It was recognized by the 1998 *Evening Standard* and the 1998 Critics' Circle Awards for best new play and the 2000 Tony Award for the best play on Broadway, as well as a profusion of criticism and commentary unmatched in his theatrical career.

The characters of *Copenhagen* are Niels Bohr, his wife Margrethe, and Werner Heisenberg. Bohr and Heisenberg were two of the twentieth century's most important physicists, colleagues and friends before the war, divided by it, since the Nazis occupied Bohr's country, Denmark. Heisenberg held a position of importance working on the German atomic program. In 1941 he visited Bohr in Copenhagen. The play is a fictionalized account of this meeting, what was intended by it, and what resulted from it.

The play begins with the three characters, all dead, reviewing the events of the past. Among other aims, this permits some necessary exposition to be transmitted quite fluently; for instance, Heisenberg speaks: "So what was Bohr? He was the first of us all, the father of us all. Modern atomic physics began when Bohr realized that quantum theory applied to matter as well as to energy. 1913. Everything we did was based on that great insight of his."[11] That speech cunningly combines character development (for Bohr is a father to Heisenberg in other ways, besides having invented the science he practices) and information for the audience. Heisenberg explains as the play begins:

> Now we're all dead and gone, yes, and there are only two things the world remembers about me. One is the uncertainty principle, and the other is my mysterious visit to Niels Bohr in Copenhagen in 1941. Everyone understands uncertainty. Or thinks he does. No one understands my trip to Copenhagen. Time and time again I've explained it. To Bohr himself, and Margrethe. To interrogators and intelligence officers, to journalists and historians. The more I've explained, the deeper the uncertainty has become. Well, I shall be happy to make one more attempt. Now we're all dead and gone. Now no one can be hurt, now no one can be betrayed. (4)

There are several possible reasons for Heisenberg's visit to Bohr. Margrethe, who is impatient with him, suggests that Heisenberg wants to show off. He does, however, discuss the possibilities of nuclear fission and what would be necessary to make a bomb. This is a somewhat complicated technical issue, involving quantities of uranium-235 and uranium-238 and the critical mass necessary for an explosion. According to Frayn's Heisenberg, he asked Bohr a different, nontechnical question: "if as a physicist one had the moral right to work on the practical exploitation of atomic energy" (36)—in other words, work on an atomic weapon. In Margrethe's crisp summary, he was asking for absolution. Or perhaps he was inviting Bohr, his mentor, to tell him *not* to build a bomb.

But there are other possibilities: perhaps Heisenberg wanted to know if the Americans were working on an atomic bomb. Bohr, though living under Nazi occupation, might have had sources of information, at least through the British, and after he escaped from Denmark he did go to the United States and work on the Manhattan Project; there he played what he says was "my small but helpful part in the deaths of a hundred thousand people. . . . Whereas you, my dear Heisenberg, never managed to contribute to the death of one single solitary person in all your life."[12] Or perhaps Heisenberg, as Bohr sometimes suspects, wanted Bohr to get word to the American scientists (many of whom were actually German Jews who had fled from Hitler) to dissuade them from making the bomb.

On his return to Germany, Heisenberg told his superiors that it would be possible to build a bomb, but he stressed the difficulty of it and the enormous quantities of uranium necessary. The project was underfunded and no bomb built. Did he deliberately discourage it? He wildly overstated the amount of uranium that would be needed. Was this too deliberate? The play emphasizes his usual care about mathematics. Frayn invites speculation: did he make a miscalculation, or did he sabotage the Nazi bomb? This remains uncertain, and that epistemological uncertainty is an adroit use, by Frayn, of a version of Heisenberg's uncertainty principle. This principle states, roughly, that it is impossible to know both the position and the velocity of a particle, and in this play it is applied to Heisenberg's own mind, though Margrethe uses his rapid skiing as a metaphor for his quicksilver thinking. Frayn makes avid and brilliant use of the available metaphors derived from modern physics: the interdependence of a phenomenon and its observer; the progressive approximation toward truth (Bohr describes Heisenberg's efforts to explain his 1941 motives as the drafts of a scientific paper); and complementarity (light may be both a particle and a wave). As Heisenberg says,

> Complementarity, once again. I'm your enemy; I'm also your friend. I'm a danger to mankind; I'm also your guest. I'm a particle; I'm also a wave. We have one set of obligations to the world in general, and we have other sets, never to be reconciled, to our fellow-countrymen, to our neighbours, to our friends, to our family, to our children. We have to go through not two slits at the same time but twenty-two. All we can do is to look afterwards, and see what happened. (77–78)

In its stagecraft, *Copenhagen* develops several trends visible over Frayn's career. Like *Here,* it is a three-person play, wherein Frayn devotes considerable effort to understanding what people mean by what they say and intuiting unspoken assumptions and hidden motives, though of course considering the possibilities of making an atomic weapon for use against civilians is of a different order of magnitude than Cath and Phil's decisions about the placement of a toy dog. Like *Clouds, Copenhagen* uses a minimal set. Most significant is the revival of a technique Frayn used in *Benefactors.* The characters both interact with each other, in a temporal placement that is the play's *past* (mostly

1941 and 1947) and in a fairly conventional dramatic style, and narrate and comment on those past actions, in a vague *present* set some time after all of them have died. The play, then, is alternatively present action and retrospection, with retrospection, recapitulation, and interrogation of the past dominant.

A typical example of the temporal fluidity is seen in this passage. Bohr and Heisenberg are acting out, and talking about, the 1941 meeting:

> BOHR: But, my dear Heisenberg, there's nothing I can tell you. I've no idea whether there's an Allied nuclear programme.
>
> HEISENBERG: It's just getting under way even as you and I are talking. And maybe I'm choosing something worse even than defeat. Because the bomb they're building is to be used on us. On the evening of Hiroshima Oppenheimer said it was his one regret. That they hadn't produced the bomb in time to use on Germany. (42–43)

Numerous reviewers have praised *Copenhagen*. Writing for the *Guardian,* Michael Billington called it a "dazzling new play . . . a logical extension of everything he has done before." Benedict Nightingale called it "one of the boldest, meatiest plays the Royal National Theater has staged this decade." Robert Butler of the *Independent* wrote: "It's a tremendous technical feat to turn a play that deals with electrons, neutrons and photons, quantum mechanics, fission and wave equations, into a totally absorbing detective thriller about precisely what two people said to one another on a 10-minute walk in 1941. This is what Michael Frayn achieves in his superb *Copenhagen.*" And, writing in the *Sunday Times,* John Peter may have made the strongest claims:

Michael Frayn's tremendous new play is a piece of history, an intellectual thriller, a work of psychological investigation and a moral tribune in full session. I use the word "tremendous" advisedly. *Copenhagen* (Cottesloe) is the work of a cultivated, sensitive and fearlessly inquisitive mind working at full stretch under the pressure of an intense moral urgency. What is at stake is the nature of human relations and the price of survival. This is a play for people who are prepared to think hard about themselves and others in the world.[13]

There were occasional protests about the amount of scientific information—in other words, suggestions that theater audiences might not want to think that hard. Frayn himself had feared that the technical language and scientific concepts involved might mean the play would not be staged.

These were the play's reviews. Later reflection, often by people who had a different professional interest in the materials of *Copenhagen*—that is, historians or scientists—raised more objections to Frayn's uses of history, particularly what seemed to some observers to be his exploitation of uncertainty to obscure Heisenberg's guilty collusion with the Nazis, establish a moral equation between Heisenberg and Bohr, or even make Heisenberg the hero. For instance, Peter Schrag wrote that the play's "very power seems to create an implicit moral equivalence between the bomb makers, Allied and German, that the circumstances of the war don't begin to justify."[14] Writing angrily in the *Chronicle of Higher Education*, Paul Lawrence Rose, author of *Heisenberg and the Nazi Atomic Bomb Project*, accused Frayn of having constructed his play on "false historical foundations that undermine its whole intellectual edifice."[15] He seems uncertain himself whether Frayn's misfeasance arose out of sympathy for Heisenberg or desire to ingratiate himself with viewers by suggesting that science is not scientific. The play, Rose complains, "exploits parallels between the questioning by humanistic postmodernists of historical facts and the questioning by constructivists of scientific facts."[16] He concludes blisteringly:

> Thanks to the play's chic postmodernism as well as the complexity of its ideas, the subtle revisionism of *Copenhagen* has been received with a respect denied to such cruder revisionism as that of David Irving's Holocaust denial. Revisionism it is, nonetheless, and *Copenhagen* is more destructive than Irving's self-evidently ridiculous assertions—more destructive of the integrity of art, of science, and of history."[17]

Thomas Powers, author of *Heisenberg's War* (overreliance on which Rose in part blames for Frayn's misinterpretations), published a reply to Rose in the *New York Review of Books*, insisting there was uncertainty about Heisenberg's role and that

> Frayn is not venting some crazy animus against Bohr; *Copenhagen* isn't an attempt to turn the tables, invite Heisenberg back into the family of science, and drive Bohr out. Frayn is restoring to the scientists of all sides something denied to them by the historians: moral autonomy—the capacity to question what they have been asked to do.[18]

In 2004 Reed Way Dasenbrock surveyed these two sides of the *Copenhagen* controversy and offered a third way. Commenting on Powers's defense, he sums up,

> In this reading, Heisenberg is defended not by Frayn presenting the truth as sustaining Heisenberg, but by Frayn presenting the truth as something which cannot be known. Thus Powers sees the play as history, as if it were history, and

praises it for its fidelity. Rose argues that it should be seen as history—that is, he shares Powers's vision of the desired relation between history and drama—but then condemns it for falling short of this idea.

Both Powers and Rose have the play wrong, or so I intend to argue, and the first step toward getting it right is to recognize that *Copenhagen* is a play and genre does exert some force here.[19]

Cushing Strout, a historian, wrote a thoughtful essay on fictionalizing history in which he questions the playwright's assertion that "recordable history cannot reach motives and intentions, so 'the only way into the protagonists' heads is through the imagination'"—this is Frayn's explanation in the postscript to the American published script, in which he discusses the historical issues at length. But, Strout points out, historians often lack access to intentions and motives and have to deduce them from available evidence.[20]

One final, and useful, result of the controversy is explained in a survey, published in *American Scientist,* of the ways playwrights use science:

Copenhagen has, in its own way, created an observer effect, leading to a reexamination of the historical record that it scrutinizes. In February [2002], a decade ahead of their stated schedule, the Bohr family unsealed, for publication, some letters to Heisenberg that Bohr drafted in the 1950s but never sent. They cast serious doubt on one of the suggestions in the play: that Heisenberg might have been reluctant to work on the bomb for moral reasons. But the new revelations do little to settle the uncertainties in the play and nothing to alter Frayn's essential points about uncertainty. In fact, some lines of Bohr's letters, such as his repeated statement "I am greatly amazed to see how much your memory has deceived you," read as if they could have been written by Frayn.[21]

Copenhagen was staged at the Cottesloe, one of the theaters in the subsidized Royal National Theatre complex on London's South Bank. While he was waiting for the Cottesloe to become available, Frayn worked on a collection of sketches that became yet another new play, which opened just two months after *Copenhagen*, called *Alarms & Excursions: More Plays Than One* (1998). This provides ample evidence that, despite his newly honed use of recent history for serious inspection of the most important philosophical and moral questions facing humanity, he was still interested in the complexly humorous interactions of farce, the delicacies of the married life, and the challenges of modern technology. (Frayn had addressed some of these in his collection of essays, *Speak after the Beep: Studies in the Art of Communicating with Inanimate and Semi-Animate Objects*, published in 1995).

Alarms & Excursions is an artfully designed and coordinated work for the stage. Designed to be performed by four actors, two men and two women, it contains eight short plays. Of these, about half are very short and little more than blackout sketches. "Glassnost" explores the dependency of a public speaker, a politician called Lady Armament, on her autocue (teleprompter) and Kevin Stoop, the man who puts the words on it, as she help-lessly reads out what Stoop scripts, including lines like these:

But if he suddenly chooses to jump it backwards. . . . And if he suddenly chooses to jump it backwards . . . then you'll hear the same thing twice over . . . then you'll hear the same thing twice over. . . . But I give you this undertaking; it will be every bit as sincere the second time around. Every bit as sincere the second time around.[22]

"Toasters" is about the more ridiculous aspects of giving toasts, especially for those who must master plates, cutlery, and folders along with their drinks; "Immobiles" puts a married couple, the wife's mother, and a German visitor arriving on a plane through a fantastic set of changes, all facilitated by use of the telephone answering machine; and "Look Away Now" is a fantasia on the stewardess's speech on an airplane, suggesting that passengers too blasé to attend to it are missing a striptease by the cabin staff. (This sketch first saw light as a column in the *Guardian*, called "Your Inattention, Please," originally published in 1994 and appearing again in *Speak after the Beep*.)

There are two longer pieces as well, cunningly intertwined. The first act of this pairing begins with "Alarms," in which two couples trying to have dinner together are tormented by the state-of-the-art electronics of the host's home. Matters begin to go wrong when the new high-tech cork-removing machine is so advanced that no one can open the wine; then the smoke alarm begins making a little noise to announce the depletion of its battery; the situation becomes more and more fraught. At one point a caller on the telephone begins leaving a message on the answering machine; but hosts John and Jocasta have so many telephones that they can't figure out which one to pick up. Conditions accelerate dizzyingly until the last stage direction: "*He listens carefully. Doorbell. Door-knocker. Hammering on door with fists. Flapping of letter-box. Buzzer. Car alarm. Police siren. The burglar alarm goes off. Curtain*" (29).

The next piece, still the first act, is the longest of the evening. Called "Doubles," it is built on the premise of two couples checking into adjacent rooms, identical though reversed, in a hotel. The action takes place on either side of the set, with complicated cross-weaving of dialogue and action. Not only are the rooms mirror images, but in some ways the couples are as well. In one room, the man uses the trouser-press; in the other, it is the woman. In one room, the woman wants to make love; in the other, it is the man. For a while, the two couples simply act side by side, but then they become aware of each other, then curious about each other. Miles has sneered at Lynn and Laurence, deciding, presumably on the basis of their accents, that they are lower class and nicknaming them Kevin and Sharon. Similarly, Laurence, pigeonholing Miles and Melanie as posh, nicknames them Nigel and Nigella. The men develop obscurely motivated hostility toward each other; both wives urge them to leave it alone. Later the wives, and then the husbands, meet their counterparts on the balcony and make common cause on the basis of gender. The interaction between the two couples is brilliantly written. As theater, "Doubles" is very delicate; Robert Butler wrote during the rehearsals that the roles of Miles and Laurence "are two of the most technically demanding roles in the West End, requiring an absolute lightness of touch."[23]

The second act begins with "Leavings," which is the continuation of "Alarms." John and Jocasta, Nicholas and Nancy, back from the emergency room (where Nancy had to be treated after injuring herself with the wine-opener), find themselves unable to bring the evening to a close. Sometimes the women will move toward the door, sometimes the men, but something always prevents a clean break, in the way that social evenings sometimes work, and as the curtain falls they are making breakfast. John comes close to voicing the theme of the entirely play when he says to Nicholas, "what you were saying . . . was that there was something unnatural about our dependence on all these machines" (88). That Nicholas denies having said it and the two begin to argue about what is natural and what is unnatural gives a linguistic turn to the evening, demonstrates the way good intentions of making a departure are easily frustrated, and illustrates once again the masculine competitiveness also visible in "Doubles."

With some exceptions, reviewers admired *Alarms & Excursions*. The recent example of the morally serious and intellectually challenging *Copenhagen* may have made the comedy seem more lightweight than it is, by contrast. The *Financial Times* reviewer, though acknowledging the humor, wrote, "The contrast with *Copenhagen*'s rigorous intellectual calisthenics could not be starker: is there, the audience seems to be being asked, no end to Frayn's talents? The answer, unfortunately, is yes, there is."[24] Benedict Nightingale related the play to *Copenhagen* by connecting both of them to Frayn's "overriding theme, which is humanity's doomed efforts to make sense of and impose order on an infinitely puzzling, unsettling world."[25] John Peter, who provided the most rapturous review of *Copenhagen* in the major British papers, called *Alarms & Excursions* "a wickedly funny take on life in the machine-driven age" and observed, astutely, that "Frayn is writing about life and living, and how living, with its props and artificial needs, keeps getting in the way of life."[26]

In 2003 Frayn returned to the broad topic under consideration in *Copenhagen,* the development of modern European history, and once again examined some of the fascinating ambiguities in that history. His focus this time was on West Germany in the 1970s, particularly on the perplexing, charismatic leader Willy Brandt, the former mayor of West Berlin who rose to be head of the Social Democratic Party and became chancellor of the German Democratic Republic. His policy of Ostpolitik led to a normalization of relations with the Soviet Union and other Communist states, including East Germany, and was a precursor to the unification of East and West Germany in the late 1980s. He won the Nobel Peace Prize in 1971 for his Ostpolitik efforts. But Brandt resigned in disgrace in 1974; the main cause was the discovery that for years one of his personal staff, Günter Guillaume, had been spying for the Communist security agencies in East Germany. Guillaume had come under suspicion before, had penetrated to his position close to Brandt almost inadvertently, and had remained there (although Brandt had asked that he be replaced) for the most mundane kinds of reasons, including staff shortages. Guillaume was convicted of espionage, along with his wife. A secondary cause of Brandt's retirement was his scandalous sex life, which began to reach public awareness only because of the Guillaume revelations.

The history and the play Frayn makes of it are rich in ironies. It was very much in the interests of East Germany to maintain Brandt in power: his policy of rapprochement benefited the state, and the unintended consequence of the espionage—the forced resignation—was recognized by East German security leaders as a disaster. Too, Guillaume, as presented in Frayn's play at least, is attracted to Brandt. He takes pride in the job he does as a personal assistant supporting the chancellor, just as he does in his other job, as a spy betraying him. As he says in *Democracy,* after his exposure:

> I let Willy down. I saw him on the news. He looked sick at heart. His first trip without me to watch over him. Wearing half of one suit and half of another! And no upturned faces! Who wrote his schedule? Who sent him on a walkabout when everyone was at home watching the football?[27]

Guillaume's duplicity and duality are echoed in various ways in the play. Germany is both one and two (East and West); Brandt comes to power by making a partnership with a rival party, forming a coalition, and Frayn seems to suggest that people are also coalitions—uneasy ones. Brandt is both the decisive hero of the German resistance, whose bold stroke brought to an end years of simmering animosity between east and west, and the man whose inability to make decisions and lack of self-discipline (about alcohol and particularly about women) proved career-ending weaknesses. Guillaume is torn in two directions, and the staging of the play illustrates this. He speaks to Brandt and the other members of the German government; but he is also, between times, speaking to Kretschmann, his East German espionage control, who stands on the other side of the stark stage.

This is another play, like *Copenhagen,* in which Frayn mixes narration with dramatic action. In a typical passage, the speeches set off by dashes are those in which Guillaume speaks to Kretschmann, commenting on the action the other speeches entail:

GUILLAUME: Anything I can do for you, Reinhard? Filing? Copying? Watering the plants?

WILKE: Thank you, Herr Guillaume. We do have secretaries

GUILLAUME: Extra pair of hands always available if you need them. No job too big or too small.

WILKE: I'm sure you have plenty to do upstairs.

GUILLAUME: —He's a little resistant to my charms. I'm not a prof or a doctor of anything like all the others.— Just popping down to Party Headquarters. Anything you want me to take? Files? Papers?

WILKE: We have messengers, Herr Guillaume.

GUILLAUME: —I'll wear him down in the end.

KRETSCHMANN: —Take your time. Don't rush it. We've waited thirteen years. We can wait a few more weeks. (8)

This dividedness, this complexity of motivation and action, explains why Frayn insists that not only "all politics is necessarily complex, since its essence is the practical resolution of differences of interest and outlook which are in principle irreconcilable. All human beings, too, are complex—but Brandt . . . was certainly more complex than most. He was certainly more complex than he seemed."[28] Another reflection on the play relates this complexity to its title: the play, Frayn told Neal Ascherson, "is about the complexity of human arrangements and how anything ever gets done. Especially inside individuals. There's a sort of democracy going on inside each one of us."[29]

Critical reactions to *Democracy* touched on several recurrent issues. One of these was Frayn's originality, or daring, in choosing to write about a period of German history in which people were not much interested. The Nazi period is what readers and viewers inexhaustibly care about; the postwar period of peace and prosperity has long seemed a stretch of boring *Gemütlichkeit*. The author addresses this matter in the published postscript to the play: "To me, I have to say, that material prosperity, that peacefulness, even that supposed dullness, represent an achievement at which I never cease to marvel or to be moved."[30] Certainly Germany's postwar resurgence, arising from utter defeat and the reduction of most of its cities to smoking rubble (the events of the play are less than thirty years after Hitler's death), is impressive. This is not to say, however, that it inherently makes for good theater; it is Frayn's wise choice of an angle (Guillaume), a major figure (Brandt), a moment, and an appropriate way of making them all into a play that produces what Ian Johns called "an award-winning sell-out" and "a complex and rewarding drama that's alert to irony and ambiguity."[31]

The ironies and ambiguities include the irony that East Germany's spying on Brandt helped to destroy its best friend in the west, and the further irony, or ambiguity, that the fruits of that spying may have been of no use to the Stasi anyway. Ironies and ambiguities exist in history; it is Frayn's strength to have noticed them, cherished them, and made a play of them.

British reviews sometimes assumed that *Democracy* contained a coded commentary on the politics of Frayn's own time. Thus Alistair Macaulay wrote, "There are even moments when cabinet-level plots sound deliberately reminiscent of the British situation today, or when the struggle to develop democracy in modern German sounds unnervingly like the current efforts to establish it in Iraq."[32] Neal Ascherson asked Frayn about this possible topical reference:

> I suggest to Frayn that *Democracy*'s picture of a Cabinet and a Chancellery busily spinning, leaking and briefing against rivals will make journalists ask an obvious question. Is this meant to be a play about Tony Blair and his Downing Street court, as much as about Willy Brandt and his devious colleagues in the Palais Schaumburg at Bonn?
>
> His answer is no, but not absolutely no. Blair isn't multiple and interesting in the way that Brandt was. You can't imagine him saying, as Frayn makes Brandt say, that "inside each of us, (there are) so many more people still, all struggling to be heard—first one voice dominates, then another."[33]

Frayn admires Blair and sees him as someone trying to get something done: in this respect, at least, like Willy Brandt.

Democracy was a success by almost any theatrical standards. It earned a long run in the West End and in New York (and a performance in Germany); in London it won the *Evening Standard* award for Best Play of the Year and the Critics' Circle award for best play. Though not uniformly praised by critics— Aleks Sierz found it dry, "an evening of intellectual pleasure rather than entertainment"—the more typical judgment was something like Paul Taylor's: "*Democracy,* Michael Frayn's complex and richly rewarding new play . . . is wonderfully alert to piquant paradoxes and ironic twists."[34] Johann Hari wrote, "Nobody could accuse *Democracy* of being unchallenging. Michael Frayn's new play is so unashamedly highbrow (like his previous play, the masterpiece *Copenhagen*) that at times he almost seems to be defying his audience to lose concentration with long, dense descriptions of the exact make-up of Willy Brandt's coalition. Amazingly, the writing is so vivid that this never happens."[35]

Alistair Macaulay's review of *Democracy* began with an observation on Frayn's work as a dramatist that ably sums up thirty-five years of writing for the theater:

Michael Frayn is the most versatile but least innocent of our playwrights, the one to whom irony in its various tones is most natural, the artist who will never wholly conceal art. Though he presents goodness, heroism, outstanding human achievement, he does so through such filters as memory, doubt, alien commentary. Deceptions, spies, multiple viewpoints abound in his work, and his narrators generally turn out to be unreliable.[36]

CHAPTER 7

Conclusion

An effort to sum up Michael Frayn's accomplishment in a short compass would be pointless and reductive. Considering the magnitude of his accomplishment in the time—nearly half a century—since he began publishing, and the diversity of work he has undertaken in that time renders an overview difficult. Readers are likely to remember his major work as his fiction and his work for the theater. From *The Tin Men* to *Spies,* Frayn's novels enact two sorts of development. One is a demonstration of his multifarious versatility. There are not many first-rate twentieth-century novels of dystopia; there are even fewer visions of what Heaven is, written by a dispassionately unreligious author, as thought provoking as is *Sweet Dreams.* His comic novels are comic in different ways, from something close to knockabout farce in *Towards the End of the Morning* to a bittersweet creation, in *The Trick of It,* that combines hilarity with gusts of sadness. It would not be obvious to a reader without any information about the author that *Headlong* and *Now You Know* could have come from the same hand.

Another sort of "development" should be noted with caution. Michael Frayn's novels have become deeper and more serious in the thirty-eight years between *The Tin Men* and *Spies.* This may be partly a consequence of the author's own maturing, or aging, and the deep-focus retrospection of *Spies* is a more plausible creation of a seventy-year-old author than one in his twenties. Nevertheless, an intelligent reader will not conclude that Frayn's humor is in inverse proportion to the thematic importance or significance of his novels. Humor is serious, too. The less antic tone of his later novels may be in proportion to the more complicated material—this is especially obvious in a book like *Headlong*—but that novel, too, has moments of brilliant comedy. Christopher Hitchens, a political writer, thinks *The Tin Men* is Frayn's masterpiece.

Something like the same "progression"—or, to put it a more neutral way, change—is detectable in his works for the theater as well. There is more pure farce in his early work, more intellection in the later, particularly in plays such as *Copenhagen* and *Look Look*. Again, there is no value judgment in this observation. And the fact that the late political plays *Copenhagen* and *Democracy*—the two works that address the most serious consequences, that probably invite the fewest laughs from the audience—are bookended around *Alarms & Excursions* should make it clear that Frayn still values farce, witty reflection on the marital relation, and cleverly worked out situations, too.

If he had never written a play or a novel, though, Michael Frayn would nonetheless be a significant figure in the literature of the postwar period in England. Before he succeeded in drama or fiction he was one of the masters of the short form in his *Guardian* and *Observer* pieces. James Fenton's praise of those works applies to his longer ones as well, but it should remind the reader that Michael Frayn the essayist is a figure of importance as well:

Michael Frayn's virtues as a comic writer were always based on an ability to evoke the instantly recognizable—the awful predicament, the common foible, the typical character. He is the funniest journalist of our time, and he is also the master of comic form. These are not merely sustained jokes. They are model essays.[1]

And, had he written neither novels, nor plays, nor essays, it is likely that he would be famous and remembered for his translations. He has become the standard translator of Chekhov's plays and the renewed popularity of that playwright is both a consequence of Frayn's elegant translations and a reason why they will remain before the public. It is impossible to judge the accuracy or delicacy of his translations without a knowledge of Russian equal to his own, but it is obvious that in translating Chekhov's *Three Sisters* and *Uncle Vanya* and *Wild Honey,* Frayn has written first-class English plays that still feel like Chekhov.

Fenton's words about the essays touch on an important point about much of Michael Frayn's work: his interest in the common foible, the typical character. In an important sense, he is the celebrator, and the inquisitor, of ordinary life. He insists that ordinary life is more unusual than people may think it is: this underlies his claim that in writing farce he is writing about real life, that farce is what human lives are like. And Frayn insists equally that extraordinary life is more ordinary than people recognize. Willy Brandt is a giant of twentieth-century history: but he is a lot like the average man, too. No man is a hero to his valet, it has been said, and this simply means familiarity breeds, if not contempt, at least an accurate or less starry-eyed valuation. Michael Frayn seeks familiarity with the real life that we all inhabit. He dramatizes it in a way that makes it funnier, more puzzling, more interesting, more philosophically significant than it feels to those caught up in it: this is true. But he values human life as it is lived by erring humans. This is why there are few, if any, villains in his works. And this is why he disclaims any intention of writing "attacks," deploring the sneering tone that enters into much literature, especially that which aspires to be satire.

His sympathy arises from an awareness of all the ways that people—most people—are trying to get things done; and an awareness that conditions frustrate them. In *Towards the End of the Morning,* Jannie Dyson observes "the chaos and the fragmentation of life!" and wonders: "what about the wrong numbers, and the garbage collecting in the garden, and the slates falling off the roof?"[2] This is what life is like, Frayn seems to say. Most human lives have more fallen slates, or spilled sardines, or missed flights, or broken fax machines, than they do moments of heroic endeavor, transcendent bliss, or tragic loss. Life is not absurd, and the good intentions and generous actions and serious undertakings of which many of his characters are capable—along with the sneaky deeds, the selfishness, the dishonesty and lovelessness of which others (or even the same characters) are equally capable—are all conditioned and constrained by entropy: these make up the picture of life so richly presented in Michael Frayn's essays, novels, and plays.

Notes

Chapter 1

1. "There's Still Life in the Old Stager: Profile: Michael Frayn," *Sunday Times* (London), January 27, 2002, I15.

2. Christopher Hitchens, "Between Waugh and Wodehouse: Comedy and Conservatism," in *On Modern British Fiction,* ed. Zachary Leader (Oxford: Oxford University Press, 2002), 53.

3. Malcolm Bradbury, *The Modern British Novel* (London: Penguin, 1993), 411.

4. Christopher Innes, *Modern British Drama, 1890–1990* (Cambridge: Cambridge University Press, 1992), 312.

5. Quoted in Benedict Nightingale, "Michael Frayn: The Entertaining Intellect," *New York Times Magazine,* December 8, 1985, 125.

6. Giles Gordon, quoted in Nightingale, "Entertaining Intellect," 125.

7. Quoted in Nightingale, "Entertaining Intellect," 125.

8. Quoted in Sarah Lyall, "Enter Farce and Erudition: Ambiguity Fires a Novelist and Playwright," *New York Times,* October 25, 1999, E1, 3. Frayn is regularly referred to as professorial or donnish. This seems to be the effect of his intellectual interests and the way he appears to interviewers: thin, reserved, thoughtful, polite, bespectacled.

9. Philip Hensher, "The Ruthless Grip of Language," *Spectator,* May 25, 2002, 39.

10. Larissa MacFarquhar, "A Dry Soul Is Best: Friendship, Espionage, and the Plays of Michael Frayn," *New Yorker,* October 25, 2004, 66.

11. Nicholas Wroe, "The Guardian Profile: Michael Frayn: A Serious Kind of Joker," *Guardian* (Manchester), August 14, 1999, Saturday Review sec., 6.

12. Shusha Guppy, "Michael Frayn: The Art of Theater XV," *Paris Review* (Winter 2003): 199.

13. Ibid., 200.

14. Michael Frayn, "Introduction," in *The Additional Michael Frayn* (London: Methuen, 2000) [pages unnumbered].

15. Ibid.

16. Humphrey Carpenter, *That Was Satire That Was: Beyond the Fringe, the Establishment Club, Private Eye, That Was the Week That Was* (London: Victor Gollancz, 2000), 168–69.

17. James Fenton, "Introduction," in *The Original Michael Frayn,* by Michael Frayn (Edinburgh: Salamander, 1983), 11.

18. Frayn, "Introduction," in *Additional Michael Frayn.*

19. Fenton, "Introduction," 11.

20. Wroe, "Serious Kind of Joker," 6.

21. Nightingale, "Entertaining Intellect," 128.

22. Michael Frayn, "Introduction," in *Plays: 2* (London: Methuen, 1991), vii.

23. Wroe, "Serious Kind of Joker," 7

24. Claire Armitstead, "Arts: Write the Same Thing Over and Over," *Guardian* (Manchester), January 31, 2002, 10.

25. Marcy Kahan, "Michael Frayn," *BOMB Magazine* 73 (Fall 2000): 59.

26. "There's Still Life in the Old Stager," *Sunday Times* (London), January 27, 2002, sec. I, 15.

27. Robert Hanks, "A Marriage between the Sheets: The IOS Profile: Michael Frayn and Claire Tomalin: Why the Whitbread Judges Should Change the Rules for Britain's First Literary Couple," *Independent on Sunday* (London), November 17, 2002, 27.

28. Harvey McGavin, "Honoured? No Thanks, Say Elite of Arts and TV," *Independent* (London), December 23, 2003, 7.

29. Guppy, "Michael Frayn," 191.

30. Nightingale, "Entertaining Intellect," 68; Robert McCrum, "Taking a Frayn Check," *Observer* (London), October 24, 1999, Review sec., 1.

31. Michael Frayn, "Introduction," in *Plays: 1* (London: Methuen, 1985), xi.

32. Julia Llewellyn Smith, "Making Sense from Nonsense," *Financial Times* (London), February 23, 2002, 3.

33. Hensher, "Ruthless Grip of Language," 39.

34. Christopher Hitchens, "The Real Thing," in *Unacknowledged Legislation: Writers in the Public Sphere* (London: Verso, 2000), 54.

35. Armitstead, "Write the Same Thing," 10.

36. Wroe, "Serious Kind of Joker," 7.

Chapter 2

1. Guppy, "Michael Frayn," 201.

2. *Listen to This: Sketches and Monologues* was also published as *Listen to This: 21 Short Plays and Sketches* (London: Methuen, 1990).

3. Michael Frayn, *Speak after the Beep: Studies in the Art of Communicating with Inanimate and Semi-Animate Objects* (London: Methuen, 1997), 162.

4. Michael Frayn, *The Day of the Dog* (London: Collins, 1962), 110.

5. Michael Frayn, *On the Outskirts* (London: Collins, 1964), 59.

6. Frayn, *Original Michael Frayn,* 180.

7. Frayn, *Speak after the Beep,* 91–92.

8. Kahan, "Michael Frayn," 55.

9. Wroe, "Serious Kind of Joker," 6.

10. Frayn, *On the Outskirts,* 73.

11. Frayn, *Speak after the Beep,* 41.

12. Frayn, *Original Michael Frayn,* 147.

13. Ibid., 163.

14. Frayn, *On the Outskirts,* 123.

15. Frayn, *Day of the Dog,* 113.

16. Ibid., 153.

17. Michael Frayn, *At Bay in Gear Street* (London: Collins, 1967), 89.

18. Frayn, *Day of the Dog,* 162.

19. Ibid., 163–64.

20. Ibid., 165–66.

21. Guppy, "Michael Frayn," 203–4.

22. Frayn, *On the Outskirts,* 148.

23. MacFarquhar, "Dry Soul Is Best," 71.

24. Frayn, *At Bay in Gear Street,* 35.

25. Frayn, *Speak after the Beep,* 151–52.

26. Quoted in Jill Dunning, "Translating: A Frayn of Mind," *ITI Bulletin,* January 2, 2003, 10–11, http://www.iti.org.uk/pages/ITIbulletin/itiBull.asp.

27. Michael Frayn, trans., "Introduction," in *Plays,* by Anton Chekhov (London: Methuen, 1988), xi.

28. Daniel Rosenthal, "Pardon My French," *Times* (London), October 2, 2001, 2, 15.

29. John Peter, "Arts: The Pitfalls of the Creative Translator," *Sunday Times* (London), June 7, 1987, 55.

30. Benedict Nightingale, "Picking Up Where Chekhov Left Off," *New York Times,* December 14, 1986, sec. II, 1

31. Michael Coveney, "Wild Honey/Lyttelton," *Financial Times* (London), July 23, 1984, sec. I, 9.

32. "Stage View: Distilling the Heady Flavor of Early Chekhov," *New York Times,* December 28, 1984, sec. II, 4.

33. Paul Taylor, "The Judgement of Paris, France," *Independent* (London), November 28, 1995, 6.

34. Andrew Porter, "Classical Music: Helen Destroyed," *Observer* (London), December 17, 1995, 11; Michael Billington, "Vive Vivette," *Guardian* (Manchester), December 13, 1005, T13; Hugh Canning, "The Critical List," *Sunday Times* (London), January 7, 1996, Culture sec., 55; Stephen Pettit, "The Critical List," *Sunday Times* (London), December 31, 1995, Culture sec., 55.

35. James Rampton, "Like a Duck to Vodka," *Independent* (London), April 19, 1996, 13.

36. Ibid.

37. Ibid.

38. Michael Frayn and David Burke, *The Copenhagen Papers: An Intrigue* (New York: Metropolitan Books, 2001), 78.

39. Robert Winder, "Hall of Mirrors," *New Statesman,* July 24, 2000, 55.

40. Aleks Sierz, "Michael Frayn: Proofs and Spoofs in the Ironic Age and Lies," *Independent* (London), May 20, 2000, 9.

41. Ibid.

42. Michael Frayn, *Constructions* (London: Wildwood House, 1974). Text references are made parenthetically.

43. Wroe, "Serious Kind of Joker," 6.

44. Frayn, *Additional Michael Frayn,* 15.

45. Hugh Herbert, "Last Laugh of a Truth Stranger Than Farce," *Guardian* (Manchester), April 16, 1990, 9.

Chapter 3

1. Wroe, "Serious Kind of Joker," 6; Smith, "Making Sense from Nonsense," 3.

2. Michael Frayn, *The Tin Men* (Boston: Little, Brown, 1965), 4.

3. Michael Frayn, *The Russian Interpreter* (New York: Viking, 1966), 7

4. Ian Johns, "From Farce to Physics and New German Politics," *Times* (London), April 19, 2004, sec. II, 15; Jane Cornwell, "Existential Trickster," *Weekend Australian* (Sydney), February 9, 2002, R08. *Scoop* is a 1938 novel by Evelyn Waugh that satirizes journalism and the newspaper business.

5. Michael Dirda quotes Drabble in "Readings," *Washington Post Book World,* September 18, 1994, 15.

6. Michael Frayn, *Towards the End of the Morning* (London: Penguin, 1969), 9.

7. Michael Frayn, *A Very Private Life* (New York: Viking, 1968), 3.

8. Frayn, *Constructions,* ¶214.

9. David Lodge, *The Art of Fiction: Illustrated from Classic and Modern Texts* (London: Penguin, 1992), 135.

10. Frayn, *Sweet Dreams* (London: Collins, 1973), 2.

11. Nicholas Tucker, "Books: High-School Heaven and Hell," *Independent* (London), September 21, 2002, 26.

12. George Hill, "Heaven, a Hell of a Place," *Times* (London), September 10, 1980, 10; Paul Taylor, "Profile: Seriously Entertaining," *Independent* (London), August 4, 1993, 14.

13. Christopher Hitchens places Frayn in this group when he calls him a "doggedly and incurably conscience-stricken bleeding-heart liberal" ("Between Waugh and Wodehouse," 53). Frayn is responding to such stereotypes in his essay on being a "luvvie" in "Your Shameful Secret," in *Speak after the Beep,* 151–54.

Chapter 4

1. Lodge, *Art of Fiction,* 23.

2. Taylor, "Seriously Entertaining," 14.

3. Tom Adair, "The Wit to Survive," *Scotland on Sunday,* November 19, 1995, 9.

4. Michael Frayn, *The Trick of It* (New York: Viking, 1989), 7.

5. Lodge, *Art of Fiction,* 23–24.

6. Michael Frayn, *A Landing on the Sun* (New York: Viking, 1991), 1.

7. Michael Frayn, *Now You Know* (New York: Viking, 1993), 1.

8. Michael Church, "This Mojo Works Good," *Independent* (London), July 23, 1995, 26.

9. Michael Billington, "Secrets behind an Open Façade," *Guardian* (Manchester), July 20, 1995, 2.

10. Michael Frayn, "Introduction," in *Plays: 3* (London: Methuen Drama, 2000), viii. Later he rewrote it as a play.

11. Michael Frayn, *Headlong* (London: Faber & Faber, 1999), 1.

12. Frayn, *Constructions,* ¶214.

13. Adam Mars-Jones, "Books: Don't Get Embroiled with a Breughel," *Observer* (London), August 22, 1999, 11.

14. Quoted in [Terence Blacker], "Harvey Porlock," *Sunday Times* (London), August 29, 1999, Books, 6.

15. Anita Brookner quoted in Blacker, "Harvey Porlock," 6; Penelope Lively, "A Brush with History," *Independent* (London), August 14, 1999, 9.

16. Shortly after his book was shortlisted, Frayn received a phone call informing him that he had also been accused of plagiarism, since *Headlong* seemed to somebody very similar to a Roald Dahl story. The source of the allegation may have been John Sutherland, chair of the Booker judges. Accusations of plagiarism are frequently part of the Booker season. Frayn writes an amusing account of this experience, claiming that having avoided "the literary life" for forty years, it caught up with him in the accusation of plagiarism. Frayn, "Brought to Book," in *Additional Michael Frayn*, 225–28.

17. S. T. Meravi, "Frayn's Fun as Fatal Flaw," *Jerusalem Post,* January 14, 2000, 13B.

18. Lively, "Brush with History," 9.

19. Randy Cohen, "A Question of Attribution," *New York Times Book Review,* August 29, 1999, 7.

20. Ibid., 8.

21. Michael Frayn, *Spies* (New York: Metropolitan Books, 2002), 108.

22. Smith, "Making Sense from Nonsense," 3.

23. Jane Cornwell, "Existential Trickster," *Weekend Australian* (Sydney), February 9, 2002, R08.

24. Frayn, *Constructions,* ¶5.

Chapter 5

1. Michele Field, "Michael Frayn," *Publishers Weekly* 237 (March 2, 1990): 65.

2. Guppy, "Michael Frayn," 203–4.

3. Michael Frayn, "Preface," *Jamie on a Flying Visit and Birthday* (London: Methuen Drama, 1990) [unpaginated].

4. Frayn, *Day of the Dog,* 162.

5. Guppy, "Michael Frayn," 191.

6. Ibid., 204.

7. Ibid.

8. Frayn, *On the Outskirts,* 59.

9. Michael Frayn, *The Two of Us: Four One-Act Plays* (London: Samuel French, 1970), 12.

10. John Wilders, "Michael Frayn (1933–)," *British Writers,* supplement 7, ed. Jay Parini (New York: Scribner's, 2002), 58.

11. Katharine Worth, "Farce and Michael Frayn," *Modern Drama* 26 (March 1983): 53.

12. Guppy, "Michael Frayn," 206–7.

13. Frayn, *Plays: 1,* 77.

14. Ibid., xii.

15. Ibid., xiv.

16. Review of *Alphabetical Order, New Statesman,* March 14, 1975, 348.

17. Frayn, *Plays: 1,* 81.

18. Ibid., xiii.

19. Ibid., 171–72.

20. Ibid., 272.

21. Karen Blansfield, "Michael Frayn (1933–)," *British Playwrights, 1956–1995: A Research and Production Sourcebook,* ed. William W. DeMastes (Westport, Conn.: Greenwood, 1996), 148.

22. Frayn, *Plays: 1,* xiii.

23. Ibid., x–xi.

24. Karen Blansfield, "Michael Frayn and the World of Work," *South Atlantic Review* 60 (November 1995): 111.

25. Leonie Caldicott, review of *Make and Break* by Michael Frayn, *Plays and Players* 27 (April 1980): 24.

26. Frayn, *Plays: 2,* vii.

27. Frayn, *Plays: 2,* x.

28. Frayn, *Plays: 2,* 126.

29. Frayn, *Plays: 2,* x–xi.

30. Blansfield, "Michael Frayn (1933–)," 149.

31. Frank Rich, "Theater: 'Noises Off,' a British Farce by Frayn," *New York Times,* December 12, 1983), C12; Michael Coveney, "Noises Off/Savoy," *Financial Times* (London), February 14, 1983, 13; Benedict Nightingale, "Farce Kicks Up Its Heels

Again," *New York Times,* December 18, 1983, sec. 2, 1; Brendan Gill, "The Theater: Civilization on the Rocks," *New Yorker,* December 19, 1983, 123.

32. Robert Brustein, "Hard and Soft Machines," *New Republic* 191 (July 9, 1984): 26.

33. Wade Harrell, "When the Parody Parodies Itself: The Problem with Michael Frayn's *Noises Off,*" in *From the Bard to Broadway: The University of Florida Department of Classics Comparative Drama Conference Papers, Volume VII,* ed. Karelisa V. Hartigan (Lanham, Md.: University Press of America, 1987), 87.

34. Worth, "Farce and Michael Frayn," 53.

35. Tom Stoppard, *Rosencrantz and Guildenstern Are Dead* (1967; New York: Grove Press, 1968), 28.

36. David Richards, "All the World's a Farce," *Washington Post,* October 16, 1983, G1.

37. Frayn, *Plays: 1,* 377.

38. Blansfield, "Michael Frayn (1933–)," 150.

39. Frayn, *Plays: 2:* 54–55.

40. John L. DiGaetani, *A Search for a Postmodern Theater: Interviews with Contemporary Playwrights* (New York: Greenwood Press, 1991), 76.

41. Guppy, "Michael Frayn," 211.

42. Frayn, *Plays: 2,* xiii.

43. Guppy, "Michael Frayn," 207.

44. Michael Frayn, *First and Last* (London: Methuen Drama, 1989), dedication.

45. Michael Frayn, *Look Look* (London: Methuen Drama, 1990), 5

46. Blansfield, "Michael Frayn (1933–)," 150.

47. Frayn, *Plays: 2,* xiii.

48. Frayn, *Plays: 3,* vii.

49. Robert Hewison, "Last Look," *Sunday Times* (London), May 6, 1990, E1.

50. Irving Wardle, "Theatre/Discovering Everybody's Face But Their Own," *Independent* (London), April 22, 1990, 21; Jack

Tinker writing in the *Daily Mail* and Milton Shulman in the *Evening Standard,* both quoted in "Critical Review of the Week," *Independent* (London), April 21, 1990, 52.

51. These are the kind of theater-goers derided in *The Day of the Dog* (162) as "the severely subnormal."

52. Claire Armitstead, "Look Look—Aldwych Theatre," *Financial Times* (London), April 18, 1990, 21.

Chapter 6

1. Michael Frayn, *Plays: 3* (London: Methuen, 2000), vii.

2. Ibid., 12.

3. Michael Billington, "Room and Bored," *Guardian* (Manchester), August 6, 1993, 12.

4. Frayn, *Plays: 3,* vii.

5. Nicholas de Jongh, *Evening Standard,* August 5, 1993, 7; James Christopher, *Time Out,* August 11, 1993, 107; both cited in Malcolm Page, *File on Frayn* (London: Methuen, 1994), 47.

6. Lindsey Duguid, "Swells of Sadness," *Times Literary Supplement* 4715 (August 13, 1993): 17.

7. Frayn, *Plays: 3,* viii.

8. Ibid., ix.

9. Ibid., 146.

10. Nicholas Lezard, "Getting Stuck in an Open Door," *Times Literary Supplement* 4819 (August 11, 1995): 18.

11. *Copenhagen* (1998; New York: Anchor Books, 2000), 5.

12. Ibid., 91. This line, in seeming to claim a moral equivalency between the two, or even a moral advantage for the Nazi Heisenberg over Bohr, the Dane who helped the Allies, has aroused strenuous and outraged protest.

13. Michael Billington, "Review: Noises Off (Very, Very Loud Ones)," *Guardian* (Manchester), May 30, 1998, 9; Benedict Nightingale, "Speculating on Science, Hitler, and the Bomb," *New York Times,* July 19, 1998, sec. II, 4; Robert Butler, "Theatre: A Masterpiece of Uncertainty," *Independent* (London), May 31, 1998,

8; John Peter, "Fiercely Felt Blast from the Past," *Sunday Times* (London), May 31, 1998.

14. Peter Schrag, "History's Heisenberg Principle," *American Prospect,* July 31, 2000, 4.

15. Paul Lawrence Rose, "Frayn's *Copenhagen* Plays Well, at History's Expense," *Chronicle of Higher Education,* May 5, 2000, B4.

16. Ibid., B4.

17. Ibid., B6.

18. Thomas Powers, "The Unanswered Question," *New York Review of Books,* May 25, 2000, 7.

19. Reed Way Dasenbroch, "Copenhagen: The Drama of History," *Contemporary Literature* 45 (Summer 2004): 221.

20. Cushing Strout, "'Two Wings of the Same Breathing Creature': Fictionalizing History," *Partisan Review* 70 (Winter 2003): 100.

21. Harry Lustig and Kirsten Shepherd-Barr, "Science as Theater: From Physics to Biology, Science Is Offering Playwrights Innovative Ways of Exploring the Intersections of Science, History, Art and Modern Life," *American Scientist* 90 (November–December 2000): 3. The reader interested in the historical/scientific argument about *Copenhagen* should also consult Michael Posner, "The Uncertainty about Heisenberg," *Queen's Quarterly* 110 (Spring 2003): 87–92; David E. Klemm, "'The Darkness Inside the Human Soul': Uncertainty in Theological Humanism and Michael Frayn's Play *Copenhagen,*" *Literature & Theology* 18 (September 2004): 292–307; August W. Staub, "The Scientist as Byronic Hero: Michael Frayn's *Copenhagen,*" *Journal of Dramatic Theory and Criticism* 16 (Spring 2002): 133–41; Duncan Wu, "Michael Frayn, *Copenhagen* (1998)," in *Making Plays: Interviews with Contemporary British Dramatists and Their Directors,* 209–50 (New York: St. Martin's Press, 2000); Steven Barfield, "Dark Matter: The Controversy Surrounding Michael Frayn's Copenhagen," *Archipelago* 8 (Autumn 2004): 80–103.

22. Michael Frayn, *Alarms & Excursions: More Plays Than One* (London: Methuen, 1998), 111.

23. Robert Butler, "It's a Complete Farce," *Independent* (London) September 20, 1998, 4.

24. "Frayn Shows the Limits of His Talent," *Financial Times* (London), September 17, 1998, 26.

25. Benedict Nightingale, "Hilarious Evening of Marital Discord and Technological Disruption," *Times* (London), September 15, 1998, Home News sec., 11.

26. John Peter, "Things That Go Ping in the Night," *Sunday Times* (London), September 20, 1998, 17.

27. Michael Frayn, *Democracy* (London: Methuen Drama, 2003), 82.

28. Ibid., 105.

29. Neal Ascherson, "What Made Gunther Grass?" *Observer* (London), September 7, 2003, 6.

30. Frayn, *Democracy,* 99–100.

31. Ian Johns, "World of Wit and Contradictions," *Australian* (Sydney), April 22, 2004, 12.

32. Alistair Macaulay, "Democracy: National Theatre, London," *Financial Times* (London), September 10, 2003, 17.

33. Ascherson, "What Made Gunther Grass?" 6.

34. Aleks Sierz, "The World Stage," *New Statesman,* November 24, 2003, 40; Paul Taylor, "First Night: Frayn's Complex and Richly Rewarding Exploration of a Man and His Myths," *Independent* (London), September 10, 2003, 4.

35. Johann Hari, "Theatre: The Best—and Worst—Way to Tackle History," *Independent on Sunday* (London), September 14, 2003, 11.

36. Macaulay, "Democracy: National Theatre, London," 17.

Chapter 7

1. Fenton, "Introduction," 11.

2. Frayn, *Towards the End of the Morning,* 232.

Bibliography

Primary Works

The Day of the Dog. London: Collins, 1962; Garden City, N.Y.: Doubleday, 1963.

The Book of Fub. London: Collins, 1963; published as *Never Put Off to Gomorrah. . . .* New York: Pantheon, 1964.

On the Outskirts. London: Collins, 1964.

The Tin Men. London: Collins, 1965; Boston: Little, Brown, 1965.

The Russian Interpreter. London: Collins, 1966; New York: Viking, 1966.

At Bay in Gear Street. London: Collins, 1967.

Towards the End of the Morning. London: Collins, 1967; repr., London: Penguin, 1969. Published in the U.S. as *Against Entropy*. New York: Viking, 1967.

A Very Private Life. London: Collins, 1968; New York: Viking, 1968.

The Two of Us: Four One-Act Plays for Two Players. London: Collins, 1970; published as *The Two of Us: Four One-Act Plays*. New York: Samuel French, 1970. Opened July 30, 1970, Garrick Theatre, London.

Sweet Dreams. London: Collins, 1973; New York: Viking, 1974.

Constructions. London: Wildwood House, 1974.

Alphabetical Order. New York and London: Samuel French, 1976. Opened March 11, 1975, Hampstead Theatre Club, London.

Donkeys' Years. New York and London: Samuel French, 1977. Opened July 15, 1976, Globe Theatre, London.

Alphabetical Order and Donkeys' Years. London: Eyre Methuen, 1977.

Clouds. London: Eyre Methuen, 1977; New York and London: Samuel French, 1977. Opened August 16, 1976, Hampstead Theatre Club, London.

Make and Break. London: Eyre Methuen, 1980; New York and London: Samuel French, 1980. Opened March 18, 1980, Lyric Theatre, Hammersmith.

Noises Off: A Play in Three Acts. London: Methuen, 1982; New York: Methuen, 1983. Opened February 21, 1982, Lyric Theatre, Hammersmith.

The Original Michael Frayn. Edinburgh: Salamander, 1983.

Benefactors: A Play in Two Acts. London and New York: Methuen, 1984. Opened April 4, 1984, Vaudeville Theatre, London.

Wild Honey: The Untitled Play. Translation/adaptation from Chekhov. London and New York: Methuen, 1984. Opened July 19, 1984, National (Lyttleton) Theatre, London.

Plays: 1. London and New York: Methuen, 1985. Includes *Alphabetical Order; Donkeys' Years; Clouds; Make and Break;* and *Noises Off.*

Clockwise: A Screenplay. London: Methuen, 1986.

Balmoral. London and New York: Methuen, 1987. Opened June 20, 1978, Yvonne Arnaud Theatre, Guilford.

Trans. *Plays,* by Anton Chekhov. London and New York: Methuen, 1988.

First and Last. London: Methuen, 1989.

The Trick of It. London and New York: Viking, 1989.

Trans. *The Sneeze: Plays and Stories,* by Anton Chekhov. London: Methuen, 1989; New York: Samuel French, 1989.

Jamie on a Flying Visit and Birthday. London: Methuen, 1990.

Listen to This: 21 Short Plays and Sketches. London and Portsmouth, N.H.: Methuen, 1990; published as *Listen to This: Sketches and Monologues.* London: Samuel French, 1990.

Look Look. London and Portsmouth, N.H.: Methuen Drama, 1990. Opened April 17, 1990, Aldwych Theatre, London.

A Landing on the Sun. London and New York: Viking, 1991.

Plays: 2. London and Portsmouth, N.H.: Methuen, 1991. Includes *Benefactors; Balmoral;* and *Wild Honey.*

Now You Know. London: Viking, 1992; New York: Viking, 1993.

Here: A Play in Two Acts. London: Methuen, 1993; New York: Samuel French, 1994. Opened July 29, 1993, Donmar Warehouse, London.

Now You Know: A Play in Two Acts. London: Methuen, 1995; New York: Samuel French, 1996. Opened July 19, 1995, Hampstead Theatre, London.

Speak after the Beep: Studies in the Art of Communicating with Inanimate and Semi-Animate Objects. London: Methuen, 1997.

Copenhagen. London: Methuen, 1998; New York: Anchor Books, 2000. Opened May 21, 1998, Cottesloe Theatre, Royal National Theatre, London.

Alarms & Excursions: More Plays Than One. London: Methuen, 1998. Opened July 15, 1998, Yvonne Arnaud Theatre, Guilford.

Headlong. London: Faber & Faber, 1999; New York: Metropolitan Books, 1999.

Celia's Secret: An Investigation (with David Burke). London: Faber, 2000; published as *The Copenhagen Papers: An Intrigue*. New York: Metropolitan Books, 2001.

Plays: 3. London: Methuen, 2000. Includes *Here; Now You Know;* and *La Belle Vivette*.

The Additional Michael Frayn. London: Methuen, 2000.

Spies. London: Faber, 2002; New York: Metropolitan Books, 2002.

Democracy. London: Methuen, 2003; New York: Faber & Faber, 2004. Opened September 9, 2003, The Royal National Theatre, London.

Secondary Works

Armitstead, Claire. "Arts: Write the Same Thing Over and Over," *Guardian* (Manchester), January 31, 2002, 10. Related to *Spies*.

Barfield, Steven. "Dark Matter: The Controversy Surrounding Michael Frayn's *Copenhagen*," *Archipelago* 8 (Autumn 2004): 80–103. Good overview of the controversy.

Blansfield, Karen. "Michael Frayn (1933–)." In *British Playwrights, 1956–1995: A Research and Production Sourcebook,* edited by

William W. Demastes, 143–57. Westport, Conn.: Greenwood Press, 1996. Authoritative comment on the plays; contains information about dates and locations of performances, including revivals, and a representative selection of reviewers' comments.

———. "Michael Frayn and the World of Work." *South Atlantic Review* 60 (November 1995): 111–28. Addresses the important use of real-life work in the plays, focusing mostly on *Benefactors, Make and Break,* and *Noises Off.*

Carpenter, Humphrey. *That Was Satire That Was: Beyond the Fringe, the Establishment Club, Private Eye, That Was the Week That Was.* London: Victor Gollancz, 2000. Places Frayn in the 1960s "satire boom."

Dasenbrock, Reed Way. "Copenhagen: The Drama of History." *Contemporary Literature* 45 (Summer 2004): 218–38.

DiGaetani, John. L. "Michael Frayn." In *A Search for a Postmodern Theater: Interviews with Contemporary Playwrights,* 73–81. New York: Greenwood Press, 1991. Some good general explanations, particularly relevant to *The Trick of It* and *Benefactors.*

Dunning, Jill. "Translating: A Frayn of Mind." *ITI Bulletin,* January 2, 2003, 10–11. http://www.iti.org.uk/pages/ITIbulletin/itiBull .asp. Tribute to Frayn's skills as a translator.

Field, Michele. "Michael Frayn." *Publishers Weekly* 237 (March 2, 1990): 65–66. Interview, for the most part about *The Trick of It.*

Guppy, Shusha. "Michael Frayn: The Art of Theater XV." *Paris Review* 168 (Winter 2003): 188–212. The best published interview with Frayn, wide-ranging and revealing.

Harrell, Wade. "When the Parody Parodies Itself: The Problem with Michael Frayn's *Noises Off.*" In *From the Bard to Broadway: The University of Florida Department of Classics Comparative Drama Conference Papers,* vol. 7, edited by Karelisa V. Hartigan, 87–93. Lanham, Md.: University Press of America, 1987. A puerile assessment.

Hensher, Philip. "The Ruthless Grip of Language." *Spectator,* May 25, 2002, 39–40.

Hitchens, Christopher. "Between Waugh and Wodehouse: Comedy and Conservatism." In *On Modern British Fiction,* edited by Zachary Leader, 45–59. Oxford: Oxford University Press, 2002. Includes some discussion of Frayn in the context of an overview of postwar comedy.

———. "The Real Thing." In *Unacknowledged Legislation: Writers in the Public Sphere,* 43–58. London: Verso, 2000. For the most part about *Headlong.*

Kahan, Marcy. "Michael Frayn." *BOMB Magazine* 73 (Fall 2000): 54–59. General interview where Frayn makes interesting comments on success and failure in his career.

Klemm, David E. "'The Darkness Inside the Human Soul': Uncertainty in Theological Humanism and Michael Frayn's Play *Copenhagen.*" *Literature & Theology* 18 (September 2004): 292–307.

Lodge, David. *The Art of Fiction: Illustrated from Classic and Modern Texts.* London: Penguin, 1992. Lodge uses *The Trick of It* as his example in the chapter on "The Epistolary Novel," 21–24.

Lustig, Harry, and Kirsten Shepherd-Barr. "Science as Theater: From Physics to Biology, Science Is Offering Playwrights Innovative Ways of Exploring the Intersections of Science, History, Art and Modern Life." *American Scientist* 90 (November–December 2000): 1–8. On *Copenhagen,* among other works where playwrights have incorporated science into drama.

Lyall, Sarah. "Enter Farce and Erudition: Ambiguity Fires a Novelist and Playwright." *New York Times,* October 25, 1999, E1, 3. Interview and profile.

MacFarquhar, Larissa. "A Dry Soul Is Best: Friendship, Espionage, and the Plays of Michael Frayn." *New Yorker,* October 25, 2004, 64–73. Good on Frayn's personality and approach to theater; a certain amount of biography and comment by friends and other observers.

McCrum, Robert. "Taking a Frayn Check." *Observer* (London), October 24, 1999, review sec., 1. Interview and profile relating to the decision on the Booker Prize for which *Headlong* was nominated.

Nightingale, Benedict. "Michael Frayn: The Entertaining Intellect." *New York Times Magazine,* December 8, 1985, 67–68, 125–28, 133.

Page, Malcolm. *File on Frayn.* London: Methuen, 1994. A useful overview, with a chapter on each of Frayn's books up to 1994, a selection of critical commentaries, and a bibliography.

———. "Michael Frayn (8 September 1933–)." In *Dictionary of Literary Biography.* Vol. 194, *British Novelists since 1960, Second Series,* 128–37. Detroit: Gale, 1998. Biography and commentary on many of the works; bibliography.

Posner, Michael. "The Uncertainty about Heisenberg." *Queen's Quarterly* 110 (Spring 2003): 87–92. About *Copenhagen.*

Powers, Thomas. "The Unanswered Question." *New York Review of Books,* May 25, 2000, 4, 6–7. A review of *Copenhagen* broadly supportive of Frayn's approach to the Heisenberg question.

Rose, Paul Lawrence. "Frayn's 'Copenhagen' Plays Well, at History's Expense." *Chronicle of Higher Education,* May 5, 2000, B4–6. A furious denunciation of Frayn, comparing him unfavorably with Holocaust denier David Irving.

Schrag, Peter. "History's Heisenberg Principle." *American Prospect,* July 31, 2000, 40–41. About *Copenhagen* and the Heisenberg controversy.

Smith, Julia Llewellyn. "Making Sense from Nonsense." *Financial Times* (London), February 23, 2002, 3. Interesting profile and interview.

Staub, August W. "The Scientist as Byronic Hero: Michael Frayn's *Copenhagen.*" *Journal of Dramatic Theory and Criticism* 16 (Spring 2002): 133–41.

Strout, Cushing. "'Two Wings of the Same Breathing History': Fictionalizing History." *Partisan Review* 70 (Winter 2003): 93–105. About *Copenhagen.*

"There's Still Life in the Old Stager: Profile: Michael Frayn." *Sunday Times* (London), January 27, 2002, I15. About the revival of Frayn's fortunes with *Spies* and a new Broadway production of *Noises Off*.

Wilders, John. "Michael Frayn (1933–)." In *British Writers*, supplement 7, edited by Jay Parini, 51–65. New York: Scribner's, 2002. A sensible and useful overview of Frayn's work.

Worth, Katharine. "Farce and Michael Frayn." *Modern Drama* 26 (March 1983): 47–53. Contains useful ideas about farce; focuses for the most part on *Noises Off*.

Wroe, Nicholas. "The Guardian Profile: Michael Frayn: A Serious Kind of Joker." *Guardian* (Manchester), August 14, 1999, Saturday Review sec., 6. Long, thorough interview and profile.

Wu, Duncan. "Michael Frayn, *Copenhagen* (1998)." In *Making Plays: Interviews with Contemporary British Dramatists and Their Directors*, 209–50. New York: St. Martin's Press, 2000. Of interest because it includes an interview with the director, Michael Blakemore, as well as playwright Frayn.

Index